Richard Acklam and Araminta Grace

going for Gold

Intermediate

coursebook

Longman

Contents

Listening	Speaking	Writing
Short extracts (multiple-choice pictures) *Listening for specific information	Discussion – family occasions *Talking about likes	Story (1): continuing a story *Brainstorming ideas *Making your writing interesting Completing a questionnaire *Short answers
Alton Towers – a recorded message (multiple choice) *Predicting before listening	Personal conversation – free time activities *Giving interesting details	Informal letter (1): describing your routine *Organising paragraphs *Using topic sentences
Things that smell Short extracts (multiple-choice pictures) Song: *Don't say you love me* (The Corrs)	Describing a photograph *Expressions with *look* (e.g. *looks tired, looks like a fun place*) *Organising general comments	Informal letter (2): describing a film or play *Organising paragraphs *Spelling
Improving your mind (neurobics) (true/false) *Listening for specific information	Describing a photograph *Speculating (e.g. *looks like, seems as if*)	Story (2): from a title *Linkers of time *Brainstorming ideas
Masks – origins and uses (note taking) *Using the introduction to predict and help understand the rest of a text *Beauty is in eye of beholder* (multiple choice)	Task – discussing statements *Giving opinions, agreeing and disagreeing	Story (3): from first sentence *Using a variety of sentence types *Using interesting vocabulary
The Internet and DotComGuy (true/false) *Computer Games Festival* – a recorded message (multiple choice)	Personal conversation – plans for the future *Ways of talking about the future	Messages and notes *Style: informal language
Martin Harrison – tattooist (note taking)	Discussion Ways of exercising *Helping your partner to contribute to the discussion	Informal letter (3): invitation *Punctuation
The same routine (note taking) *Identifying facts and opinions	Comparing photographs – describing strange buildings *Prepositional phrases of place (e.g. *in the background*)	Transactional letter (1): recommending which place to visit *Organising a transactional letter *Linkers of contrast
Bilingual kids (multiple choice) Song: *When you say nothing at all* (Ronan Keating)	Task – deciding where to go *Making suggestions and negotiating	Discursive composition: learning English by computer *Organising a discursive composition *Linkers of addition
Extracts about incidents with animals (multiple matching)	Task – coming to a decision *Making a decision and giving reasons	Report (1): popular pets *Organising a report *Linkers of consequence
Discussion of a newspaper article (true/false)	Discussion – survival situations *Giving advice	Informal letter (4): about a frightening or dramatic experience *Organising paragraphs *Style: informal language
Childhood memories (multiple matching)	Comparing photographs (memories) *Ways of comparing and contrasting	Story (4): from first sentence *Editing your writing *Linkers of time
Visiting Sydney – tour guide (note taking) *Away from home* (true/false)	Comparing photographs *Organising general and specific points	Article: for a travel magazine *Organising an article *Planning and editing your writing
Rachel Carson, eco-warrior (note taking) Song: *Feelin' so good* (Jennifer Lopez)	Task and discussion – environmental issues *Pausing before speaking and asking for someone else's opinion	Transactional letter (2): planning a weekend *Organising a transactional letter *Linking paragraphs
Food and drink: short extracts (multiple choice) *Identifying content, relationship or attitude	Task and discussion – issues about food and eating *Review of suggestions, decisions, pausing and asking for opinions	Report (2): food preferences *Organising a report *Style: formal language

A question of family

A — Sophie Dahl — Roald's granddaughter

C — Nick Moss — Kate's brother

B — Kate Moss

D — Roald Dahl

Reading 1

1 There are some family connections between the people in these photos. What do you think they are?

2 Picture A is of the supermodel, Sophie Dahl. With another student, write down three questions you would like to ask her.

3 Now look at the questions in italics in the article. Were any of them the same as your questions?

Vocab check

Supermodel in the hot seat

The model Sophie Dahl, 20, is the granddaughter of the children's writer Roald Dahl. She is quite unusual because, for once, we have a supermodel who is bigger than the average size. Sophie works for model agency Storm. She has been in a number of top fashion magazines including *Elle*, *Vanity Fair* and *Italian Vogue*. She kindly agreed to answer some questions from our readers.

How did you start modelling? Is it something you always wanted to do? (Danni Fielding, Bristol)

I actually wanted to be a writer but then I was spotted on the street. I was crying after having a huge fight with my mother and this woman said to me, 'Let me make you into a supermodel' and I said, 'OK.'

What do you do with all the hours between fashion shows? (Lisa Stevenson, King's Lynn)

Read a lot, and drink endless cups of tea.

Do you exercise? If so, what do you do and where? (Emily, Nuneaton)

I work out with a trainer three times a week.

Do you believe in marriage? (Debbie Penrose, Winchester)

Yes! But only for love.

Who is your ideal man? (Chris and Tony, Liverpool)

Somebody who makes me laugh a lot, who thinks I look fantastic with unwashed hair – and who'll send me flowers. Basically, no one I know, unfortunately.

What was the last film and the last pop group you went to see? (Sara Peters, Nottingham)

I went on a date to see *Armageddon* in New York. The film was dreadful and the date not much better. The last group I saw were the Beastie Boys and they were fantastic!

What memories do you have of your grandfather? Have you read any of his books – and if so, which ones are your favourites? (Paula, Chester)

I miss him terribly. He was extraordinary. We used to talk about books a lot. I made him laugh. My favourite book by him is *The BFG*, which is actually about me!

What do you think you'll be doing five years from now? (Chrissie Hagan, Norwich)

Hopefully, I'll be happy and extremely rich, so I won't have to work! I'll also be married to an amazing guy, making pasta somewhere in southern Italy, surrounded by my friends.

4   Read the complete article and decide if these statements are true or false.

1 Sophie Dahl is a typical supermodel. *F*

2 She didn't always want to be a model. *T*

3 She has quite a lot of time between fashion shows. *T*

4 She exercises on her own. *F*

5 She has found her ideal man. *F*

6 She didn't like the pop group she saw recently. *F*

7 She really liked her grandfather. *T*

8 She hopes she won't be working as a model in five years' time. *T*

5   Work with another student. Choose three of the questions in the article which are relevant to you. Then, ask and answer them together.

⟶ *But you're not losing a daughter, we're going to live here.* *ask students what this mean*

Vocabulary 1: meaning from context

1   Discuss these questions with a partner.

1 Which of these things have you read recently in English?
   A all or part of a book
   B an article in a newspaper
   C a text in this coursebook
   D something else

2 When you read in English, do you usually
   A understand every word?
   B understand most of the important words?
   C understand about half of the words?
   D understand only a few of the words?

3 What do you do when you don't understand a word?
   A just continue reading and not worry about it
   B stop every time and look up every word in a dictionary
   C stop sometimes and look up important words in a dictionary
   D stop sometimes and try to work out the meaning of important words from the context

4 What is good or bad about each of the possibilities in question 3 above?

   Example: *It's not good to look up every word in a dictionary because not every word is important.*

2   Look at the article on page 4 again. Try to work out the meaning of the six highlighted words from their contexts.

1 Look at the highlighted words. Decide what part of speech (noun, verb, adjective, etc.) each one is.

2 Look at the words and sentences before the highlighted words and after them. Think what the highlighted words might mean.

3 Now decide which of the words in the box below has the closest meaning.

   Example: actually – *in fact*

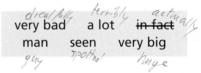

very bad	a lot	~~in fact~~
man	seen	very big

really / terribly / actually / guy / spotted / huge / guessing word meaning

3   Find something in English to read, e.g. a newspaper article or a page from a book. *homework*

1 Read it on your own, without a dictionary. Highlight any words you don't understand.

2 Decide which of the highlighted words are important in order to understand the whole article or story.

3 Look at the important words again. Try to work out the meaning from the context. Use any clues you can find in the sentences around the word.

4 Be prepared to report back to the class. Say which words you chose and how you worked out the meaning.

Grammar 1: questions (1)

1   Complete each of these questions with one of the question words in the box.

Example: *What* was the last film you went to see?
Who is your ideal man?

> What (x3)   Where   When   Who
> Whose   Why   How   How much
> How many   How often   How long

1 A: ....*What*............ is your surname?   B: Smith.

2 A: ....*How*............ do you spell that?   B: S-M-I-T-H.

3 A: ....*Where*............ are you living at the moment?
   B: In Manchester, with my parents.

4 A: ....*What*............ do you do?   B: I'm a student.

5 A: ....*How many*........ brothers and sisters have you got?
   B: One brother and one sister.

6 A: ....*How often*..... do you go to the cinema?
   B: About once a month.

7 A: ....*When*............ did you last see a band live?
   B: Last weekend.

8 A: ....*How long*.... have you been learning English?
   B: Nearly three years.

9 A: ....*Why*............ are you learning English?
   B: So I can get a good job.

10 A: ....*How much*.... does it cost to travel to your
   school from your home by public transport?
   B: About £2.

11 A: ....*What*............ country would you most like to
   go on holiday to?   B: Mexico.

12 A: ....*Who*............ is one of your favourite actors at
   the moment?   B: Ben Affleck.

13 A: (In your family) ...*Whose*............ views do you most
   respect and listen to?   B: My grandmother's.

▶ Grammar reference 1.1 p. 136

2

1 Listen to three different people answer the
   first two questions in Exercise 1. Write down
   the surnames with the correct spelling.

2 Compare your answers with another student.

1 Aitchison   /ˈeɪtʃəsən/ ˈɛtʃəsən
2 Roxburgh   /rɒksbərə/ /rɒksbrʌ/
3 Olearski   /pliˈaːskɪ/

3   Check you can pronounce the alphabet in English.
Then choose three words you have learnt recently
and ask another student to spell them.

Example:
Student A *How do you spell 'occupation'?*
Student B *O-DOUBLE C-U-P-A-T-I-O-N.*

3   Match the questions in Exercise 1 to the topics
below where possible. (Not all of them will apply.)

Example: home town – *Where are you living at the
moment?*

- home town
- school
- job
- free time
- holidays
- learning English
- family

4   Write one more question for each of the
topics in Exercise 3.

5

1 Now ask another student all your questions and
   make a note of the answers. (Ask them to spell
   their answers where necessary.)

2 Show your partner the answers. Are they all
   written correctly?

Listening

1

1 You will hear a girl talking about her family.
   Before you listen, look at the pictures and describe
   what you can see. How are they different?

How big is her family?

2 Now listen. How many brothers has she got?
   How many sisters?

3 Which picture matches her description? Did you
   have to understand every word to decide?

2   Look at questions 1–5. You will hear five more conversations. Before you listen, read the questions and look at the pictures. What do you need to listen for?

1   What's the time?

the time

A   B   C

2   What's Sally buying her dad for Christmas?

presents

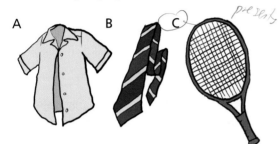

A   B   C

3   What are they doing tonight?

activities

A   B   C

4   What does Claire's boyfriend look like?

description of a person

A   B   C

5   How does Kevin usually get to school?

way of getting to school

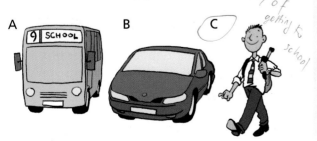

A   B   C

So most days (maest)

3   Listen and put a tick (✓) under the correct pictures. You will hear each conversation twice.

Vocabulary 2: family and friends

1   Look at Paula's family tree. Work with another student. Tell them what differences there are between this family and your family.

Work in pairs

Example: *Paula only has one brother. I have three brothers.*

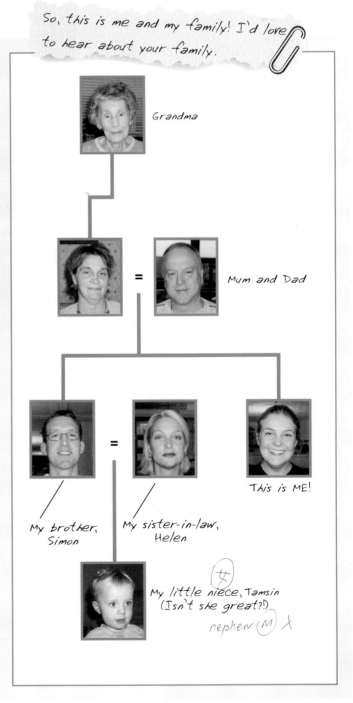

So, this is me and my family! I'd love to hear about your family.

Grandma

Mum and Dad =

My brother, Simon   My sister-in-law, Helen   This is ME!

My little niece, Tamsin (Isn't she great?!)   *nephew (M)*

2   Complete these sentences with the names of family members in the box.

Example: My wife's father is my *father-in-law*.

> grandfather   aunt   cousin
> sister-in-law   ~~father-in-law~~
> niece   widow   stepmother

1   My aunt and uncle's child is my ...*cousin*

2   My father's father is my ...*grandfather*

3   My brother's daughter is my ...*niece*

4   My father remarries, so then I have a ...*stepmother*

5   My brother's wife is my ...*sister-in-law*

6   My mother's sister is my ...*aunt /aint/*

7   If my husband dies I become a ...*widow*

3   Say what you think are the male/female equivalents for each of the words in the box in Exercise 2.

Example: father-in-law – *mother-in-law*

widower (M)
nephew (M)
uncle (M)

4   Write down the names of the people in your family who are the most important to you. Show the names to another student and explain who the people are and why they are important to you.

5   Read these questions. Check you understand them. Then discuss your responses with other students.

1   What do you think are the advantages and disadvantages of being an only child?

2   Are you close to your grandparents? Do you think grandparents should live with their families?

3   Who is your closest friend? How did you meet them originally? How long have you been friends? What do you value most about them?

Speaking

1   Look at the photograph and tell another student if you like this kind of family occasion. Give reasons.

Example: *Yes, I like family meals because my brother comes home for them. He left home last year and I don't see him often.*

2   Listen to Katia and Tomek discussing their views. Who particularly likes this type of occasion?

3

1   Listen again. Complete the expressions below which Katia and Tomek use to say what they like.

1   I ...*love*... it especially because I can see my niece.

2   I ...*quite like*... them, but my mother gets quite anxious.

3   I ...*really like*... that too. It's all good fun.

2   Listen and repeat the sentences after the recording.

4   Now, talk with another student about the kinds of things you like to do with your family and the kinds of things you don't like to do.

Writing 1: short answers

1   A market research company has sent you this questionnaire to find out about families and family life. You have agreed to complete it. Read through all the questions and make sure you understand them.

FAMILY QUESTIONNAIRE

Full name: (1) ....

Title: **Mr/Mrs/Miss/Ms/Dr** (delete as appropriate) (2)

Home address (including post code):
(3) ....
....

Telephone number: (4) ....

Nationality: (5) ....

Date of birth (day/month/year): (6) ....

Present occupation: (7) ....

How many brothers and sisters do you have?
(8) ....

Do you still live with your parents? (9) ....

Which member of your family are you closest to?
(10) ....

Are you closer to your family or your friends?
(11) ....

How often do all the members of your family come together? On what occasions?
(12) ....

Signature: (13) ....

2

1 Look at the way two people have completed part of the questionnaire. Which one is good? Which one is not?

Extract A

Nationality: (5) *I am italyan*.....................................

Date of birth (day/month/year): (6) *I born on 15th august 1985*...

Present occupation: (7) *I am a student. I am in my last year*...
at secondary school.

Extract B

Nationality: (5) *Italian*.............................

Date of birth (day/month/year): (6) *15/8/1985*.........

Present occupation: (7) *School student*..............

2 What differences do you notice between the two extracts? Think about the following:
● punctuation
● spelling
● grammar
● using complete sentences.

▶ Writing reference (Spelling) p. 151 *etymology e.g.* *homophones same sound*

3   You are going to complete the form for yourself. First, make a note of your possible answers on a separate piece of paper.

4   Show another student the answers you are thinking of writing and look at theirs. Do you notice any problems with their answers?

5   Now complete the form.

Complement with Murphy BLU

Grammar 2: indirect questions *yes*

A

What's your full name? Do you still live with your parents?

B

Could you tell me what your full name is? I'd also like to know if you still live with your parents.

1   The pictures above show someone asking a stranger in the street questions from the Family Questionnaire on this page. Answer these questions.

1 In which picture are the questions more polite?

2 What differences do you notice between the questions in each picture?

▶ Grammar reference 1.2 p. 136

2

1 Now, look at the questionnaire on page 9 again. Write direct questions where necessary (where there is no question written already).

Example: Full name – *What's your full name?*

2 Now change all the direct questions into indirect questions.

Example: What's your full name? – *Could you tell me what your full name is?*

3 Ask another student the indirect questions.

4 Here are some different situations. Roleplay them with another student. Use indirect questions where possible.

Example: 1
> **Student A** *Excuse me. Could you tell me if you have any English grammar practice books?*
> **Student B** *Certainly, they are over here, next to the dictionaries.*
> **Student A** *Thank you very much.*

1 You are in a bookshop. You want to know if they have any English grammar practice books. Ask the shop assistant.

2 You are in a shop. You are looking at some watches. You see one you like but there is no price marked. Ask the shop assistant.

ROLE PLAY
WORK IN PAIRS

3 You are interested in seeing a film called *Heartbreak* at a local cinema. Ring the cinema and ask about the price and times of the film.

Reading 2

1 Roald Dahl is a famous writer of children's books. The extract below comes from his book *The BFG* (Big Friendly Giant). The young girl in the story is based on his granddaughter, Sophie Dahl. Before you read, say what you think the words below in bold mean. Then check your ideas in an English–English dictionary.

1 Her grandfather sat in a comfortable armchair after lunch and **dozed off**. *= fall asleep*

Vocab Check

2 Ben is **hiding** somewhere in the garden and we can't find him!

Adj.   Noun
Vocabulary check
V   Noun
check Vocabulary

3 She **whispered** his name in my ear so no one else could hear.

honomatopeic

4 In the past, a **witch** was supposed to ride on a broomstick and have a black cat!

5 Mary **leaned** out of the window and waved to her friend in the street below. *moved/bent her body*

6 It was dark and Simon was feeling nervous. Suddenly he **froze**! What was that noise? *stopped suddenly to a still position*

2 Now read the extract. Do you think it is a good start to a children's book? Why?/Why not?

The witching hour

1 Sophie couldn't sleep. The other children in the dormitory had been asleep for hours. Sophie closed her eyes and lay quite still. She tried very hard to doze off. It was no good. The house was absolutely silent. The window behind the curtain was wide open, but nobody was walking on the pavement outside. No cars went by on the street. Sophie had never known a silence like this. Perhaps, she told herself, this was what they called the witching hour.

2 The witching hour, somebody had once whispered to her, was a special moment in the middle of the night when every child and every grown-up was in a deep, deep sleep. At this time, all the dark things came out from hiding and had the world to themselves.

3 Sophie decided to get out of bed and close the gap in the curtains. When she reached the curtains, Sophie hesitated. She really wanted to get under them and lean out of the window to see what the world looked like now that it was the witching hour. She listened again. Everywhere it was completely still.

4 Sophie wanted to look out so badly that, in the end, she couldn't stop herself. Quickly, she went under the curtains and leaned out of the window. In the silvery moonlight, the village street she knew so well seemed completely different. Everything was pale and ghostly and milky-white.

5 Sophie looked further and further down the street. Suddenly she froze. *There was something coming up the street on the opposite side.*
It was something black …
Something tall and black …
Something very tall and very black and very thin.
WHO?

6 It wasn't a human. It couldn't be. It was four times as tall as the tallest human. It was so tall its head was higher than the upstairs windows of the houses. Sophie opened her mouth to scream, but no sound came out. Her throat, like her whole body, was frozen with fright.

3 Decide which paragraph in the story each of these pictures illustrates.

A *8/2*
B *6/4*
C *1*
D *3*

4 All the statements below are false in some way. Read the story again and say why.

Example: 1 *Sophie was not asleep.*

1 All the children were asleep.
2 It was completely quiet except for the sound of whispering. *No whispering; all asleep*
3 Sophie opened the curtains. *she went underneath*
4 It was quite dark in the village and she couldn't see much. *moonlight*
5 Sophie was so scared that she couldn't stop screaming. *"no sound came out"*

Writing 2: story (1)

1 Here are three possible continuations of the story on page 10. Which is the most interesting? Why?

1 It turned. It looked at Sophie. It smiled.
2 It turned. It looked straight at Sophie. To her amazement, it smiled.
3 Then, suddenly, it turned and looked straight at Sophie. 'This is the end,' thought Sophie. However, to her amazement, it smiled.

► Writing reference (Making your writing interesting) p. 150

2

1 Work with another student. You are going to write the next part of the story. Read the outline and the following questions.

A The BFG wants to be friends with Sophie.
Why? How does she feel about that?

B The BFG is lonely.
Why? What is his everyday life like? Does he have any friends? If so, who are they?

C The BFG has a problem.
What? What are the possible solutions to the problem? What is he going to do about his problem?

D Sophie decides to help the BFG.
Why? How will she help him?

E Sophie and the BFG go off on an adventure together.
When do they leave? Where do they go? What does she take with her? What adventure do they have?

F It all ends happily.
What happens? Do Sophie and the BFG remain friends?

2 Answer the questions with notes.

Example:
1 The BFG wants to be friends with Sophie.
Why? *Because he thinks she is brave and that she can help him.*
How does she feel about that?
Nervous but interested.

► Writing reference (Planning your writing) p. 152

3 Now write the next part of the story (about 80 words). Use your notes and the outline below. Begin with Sentence 3 from Exercise 1.

Outline
Paragraph 1 A and B
Paragraph 2 C and D
Paragraph 3 E
Paragraph 4 F

4 Show your writing to another pair of students and look at theirs. Have they used:

● interesting vocabulary? See Writing reference (Making your writing interesting) p. 150.
● correct punctuation? See Writing reference (Punctuation) p. 148.

5 Write your final version, making any improvements necessary.

► Unit test 1: Teacher's Book

UNIT 2 Time out

Alton Towers
Where The Magic Never Ends!

1 Work with other students. Describe what you can see in the pictures. Have you ever been on anything like this? If so, what was it like?

2

⚡ When you listen to a recording in English, try to predict what it is about. This will make it easier to understand.

You are going to hear a recording about a famous British theme park called Alton Towers. Before you listen, talk to another student. Tell them about a theme park, museum or other interesting place that you have visited. Answer any of these questions that you can.

1 Where is it?

2 What can you see or do there?

3 Did you enjoy it? Why?/Why not?

4 Does it have a shop? If so, what can you buy there?

5 Is there a café or restaurant there? If so, what is it like?

6 When is it open?

7 How much does it cost to go in?

3 You will now hear a recorded message about Alton Towers. Put a tick (✓) in the correct box for each question.

1 Who is Alton Towers designed for?
A teenagers ☐
B older people ☐
C the whole family ☑

2 In the grounds of Alton Towers
A there are some old buildings. ☑
B you can see only very new buildings. ☐
C they are building some shops. ☐

3 The following are rides at Alton Towers:
A Nemesis, Oblivion and Ug Land ☐
B Oblivion, Ug Land and Corkscrew ☐
C Nemesis, Oblivion and Corkscrew ☑

4 At Alton Towers, more relaxing ways to spend your time include
A visiting a museum. ☐
B walking around the gardens. ☑
C going up in a balloon. ☐

5 Daily closing times at Alton Towers
A are always the same. ☐
B depend on the weather. ☐
C vary according to the time of year. ☑

6 You can't use a credit card if you book
A by post. ☑
B by telephone. ☐
C in person. ☐

Grammar 1: present simple

1   Match the verbs in bold in sentences 1–4 to each of the categories A–D below.

C 1 My dad **takes** us to a different theme park every year.

D 2 Sally **lives** in Florida near an amazing theme park.

A 3 **Do** you **know** when the new ride will be open?

B 4 First, they **lock** you into your seat. Then the ride **begins**.

3 A verbs not used in the continuous

4 B to describe processes

1 C to describe habits

2 D to describe permanent situations

> **! Watch Out**) state verbs
> *non in -ing*
>
> Which of these sentences is not correct? Why?
>
> 1 a) I don't understand what you mean.
>   ✗b) I'm not understanding what you mean.
>
> 2 a) She loves her new computer.
>   ✗b) She's loving her new computer.

► Grammar reference 2.2 p. 137

2   Complete the following text with verbs from the box in the present simple.

.take   eat   practise   spend
not drink   listen   go   travel
not dream   wake   not practise   like

3   The words in italics in the sentences below are adverbs of frequency. In two of the sentences they are in the wrong position. Decide which the two sentences are and where the adverbs of frequency should be.

1 We *usually* go to the north of Spain for our summer holidays.

2 They *always* are late!   *they are always late*

3 I *sometimes* go swimming before school.

4 Is he *often* so rude?

5 She *occasionally* lets me borrow her bike.

6 *Never* I have toast for breakfast.   *I never have*

4   Write six complete sentences. Use the sentence beginnings on the notepad below.

Example: *My dad often plays tennis at the weekend.*

high frequency

I
My best friend
My mum/dad
My brother/sister

5 always...
4 usually ...
3 often ...
2 sometimes ...
1 occasionally ...
0 never ...

low frequency

A day in the life of a tennis star

She (1) _spends_ nine months a year on the international tennis circuit. She won her first title when she was 17.

My alarm (2) _goes_ off at 8am. I (3) _take_ a shower four times a day, but the first one in the morning is the important one. It (4) _wakes_ me up after the ten hours I sleep every night.

Breakfast is cereal, yoghurt, toast and honey and a big glass of milk. I (5) _don't drink_ coffee, and I only occasionally drink tea. For lunch I (6) _eat_ a lot of pasta and salads.

I (7) _practise_ on court for two and a half hours every morning and another two hours in the afternoon. I (8) _don't practise_ on Saturday afternoons and Sundays.

My only luxury is clothes. I like getting dressed up and I have money, so if I see something I like by Armani or Chanel, I buy it. I (9) _like_ fast cars, too.

My favourite time of day is around 5 p.m., when I'm in my room. I (10) _listen_ to Moby or Travis.

I (11) _travel_ everywhere with my mother and Roland, my dog. I'm usually in bed by about 10 p.m. I (12) _don't dream_ much, but if I do it's about a tennis tournament.

5   Ask another student *How often do you ...?* and put a tick (✓) in the correct box.

Example:
Student A *How often do you get up before 6 a.m.?*
Student B *Never!*

in pairs

	never	occasionally	sometimes	often	always
get up before 6 a.m.					
sing in the shower					
have coffee for breakfast					
read in bed before you go to sleep					
listen to music while you do your homework					
do the washing-up					
go to a film during the week					
wear jeans at the weekend					
watch TV in the morning					

6   Tell other students about the person you interviewed.

Example: *Sonia never gets up before 6 a.m.*

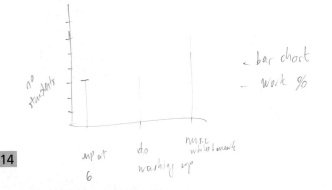

Vocabulary 1: free time

1   Match the verbs on the left with the activities on the right.

Example: going to – *the cinema*

Do you like ...

going to   jogging? ☐ —
playing   football? ☐ —
collecting   stamps? ☐
going   the cinema? – ☐
taking   table tennis? ☐ – ☐
                photographs? ☐ —
                chess? ☐
                the guitar? – – ☐
                museums? – ☐ —
                basketball? ☐ – –
                camping? ☐ –
                the piano? – ☐ —

2   How many syllables do the words on the right have? Which syllable is stressed?

Example: jogging – *2 syllables – jogging*

3

1 Complete the following sentences with a verb from Exercise 1 in the correct form.

Example: I'd like to ...*go*........... to the cinema tonight.

1 I'd like to ...*play*........ basketball for my school team.

2 I ....*took*..... lots of photographs on my last holiday.

3 I started ...*playing*... the guitar this summer.

4 I think ....*collecting*...... stamps is the most boring hobby in the world!

5 I like ...*playing*..... chess on my computer.

(handwritten: nǐ hǎo mā? 女子 中国字 中国人 中国文 明)

6 I sometimes ....*go*........ jogging with a group of my friends in the morning.

7 My family ....*went*.... camping in France last summer.

8 I could ......*play*.... the piano quite well when I was thirteen.

2 Tell another student how many of the sentences are true for you.

Example: *The first sentence is definitely true. I'd really like to play basketball for my school team!*

4 Work with another student. Can you think of any other words to go with the verbs on the left in Exercise 1?

Example: going to – *pop concerts*

5 Now tell your partner which activities you enjoy. Your partner should ask you two questions about each activity.

Example:
Student A *I like playing football.*
Student B *How often do you play?*
Student A *Twice a week.*
Student B *Who do you play with?*
Student A *I usually play with some friends who live near me.*

Speaking

1 Look at the picture of Sally below and read the text. What is she talking about? *tennis*

2 Complete the text with words from the box.

exercise	game	started	member
times	outdoors	play	doing

3 Listen and check your ideas.

4 In which order does she talk about the following things?

when and how often she does it	2
why she likes it	5
where she does it	4
how long she has been doing it	1
how she first became interested in it	3

5 Prepare to tell another student about your favourite free time activity. Make notes about each of the areas in Exercise 4.

6 Now tell another student. Try to speak continuously for at least one minute. *in pairs IN PAIRS*

I've been (1) ...*doing*.. it seriously for about two years now. In the summer, I play at least three (2) ...*times*.. a week and sometimes more. I play in winter as well, but not as much. The weather can be a problem.

I (3) ...*started*.. playing after my brother asked me to play with him and some friends. He even gave me his old racket. Now I'm a (4) ...*member*.. of a local club, and there are always people at the club who want to (5) ...*play*...... .

Why do I like it so much? Well, I love being (6) ...*outdoors*.. I really like running around and I think getting (7) ...*exercise*.. is very important. But most of all I love being able to do it with other people. It's such a friendly (8) ...*game*..!

15

Reading

1 What is the best film you have seen recently? Why did you like it?

2 These people would all like to go and see a film. On page 17 there are descriptions of eight films. Decide which film (A–H) would be the most suitable for each person or family (1–5). (The first one has been done for you.)

Example: *1 H*

As you read about each person, highlight or underline any important words or phrases. As you read about each film, look for parallel words or phrases that link the book to a particular person.

1 *H* *funny laugh*

Cathy and Jody have had a bad week at school. They'd like to see a comedy or something that will cheer them up.

2 *E* *policeman*

Jeremy is a university student who wants a break from his studies. He particularly likes crime thrillers.

3 *A* *sorcery magical powers*

Sarah Jane loves any kind of fantasy story. She has read lots of books about witches and wizards but can't get enough of them!

4 *D* *Adventure, sea*

The Dobson family want to see a film together. They all like adventure stories and Mum especially likes anything to do with the sea.

5 *B* *horror, tension, suspense*

Rita's two nieces (12 and 14) are coming to stay for the weekend. She wants to take them to something they'll enjoy. Apparently they love being scared!

3 Which two films from Exercise 2 would you be most interested in seeing? Why?

A *Harriet Hargreaves and the Sorcerer's Revenge*

3 An exciting story of a young girl who lives with her horrible stepfamily but then gets sent to Pootrot School of Sorcery and discovers she has magical powers. A rollercoaster ride of friendship and adventure which leads her to discover the truth behind 'the Sorcerer's Revenge'!

B *The Other Side*

5 A horror story with a difference. Filled with tension and suspense, this is the story of a young woman and her two children living alone in an old castle in Scotland just after the war. All is well until they take on three new servants and then everything changes.

C *Bogdoon*

This video puts the classical tale of Bogdoon on the big screen, and we are transported into a world of talking trees, grumpy rabbits and cats with attitude! Amazing animation and a heartwarming story – definitely one that the younger members of the family will love and demand to see again and again!

D *Pirate!*

4 Experience life with some of the wildest men of the ocean as they look for new islands, adventure and treasure. Action, romance and some dramatic scenes of storms at sea.

E *The Inside Story*

2 Mike Firkin is a policeman, working undercover. He's rising up the ranks of the New York Mafia. But his boss, Captain Carstairs is worried. Mike's getting too good at his job. Whose side is he really on?

F *Space Invader*

Follow the adventures of the spaceship *Sun Seeker* as she travels deep into the galaxy on a mission to help restore inter-galactic peace. A first-rate cast of actors and an excellent story help make this the science fiction movie of the year.

G *Love Divides*

Anita and Salman come from two very different Indian families. One day, they meet by chance in a park. Soon they fall in love, but then they have to face the reality of their situation. Their families are totally against the relationship. What will they do?

H *Party Time 2*

1 The hysterically funny follow up to *Party Time 1*. More laughs as we follow the lives of a group of friends in their final year at the strangest American high school you are ever likely to encounter. *comedy*

cheer them up

Vocabulary 2: recording words

1 How do you remember new words that you learn in your English class? What systems do you have? Discuss with other students.

2 Look at these different ways of recording vocabulary in a vocabulary notebook. Which of them have you used?

1 Translation

*horror – orrore
action – azione
romance – sentimentale*

2 Short English–English explanations

suspense: feeling you have when you are waiting for something exciting to happen

3 Dictionary style

*grumpy: /ˈgrʌmpi/ adjective
grumpier, grumpiest If someone is grumpy, they show that they feel slightly angry or annoyed: I'm feeling grumpy because I'm tired.*

etymology = origin = derivation

4   Pictures

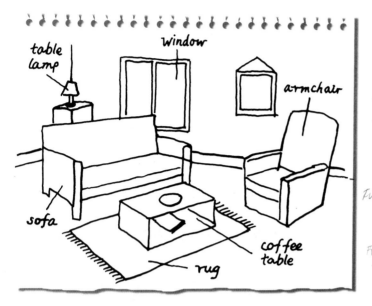

5   Mind maps

6   Grids

Job	Place of work	Responsibilities
nurse	hospital	looking after people who are ill or injured
accountant	office	Keeping/checking financial records
chef	restaurant kitchen	organising preparation of meals

3   Look at the previous *Reading* section. Are there any new words you would like to record in your vocabulary notebook? Decide how you are going to record them. When you have entered them in your notebook, show another student.

Grammar 2: continuous or simple?

1   Listen and complete the gaps in the following conversation.

T   Simon   What ..are.. ..you.. ..doing..? —Temp.

T   Katrina   I ..am.. ..reading.. about a new cinema complex. Temp

T   Simon   Are ..you.. ..thinking.. of going? —Temp

FA   Katrina   Yes, maybe this weekend. What ..are.. ..you.. ..doing.. on Saturday? Would you like to come?   FUT. ARRANGEMENT

FA   Simon   Yes. Why not? I ..am.. ..not.. ..doing.. anything else!   FUTURE ARRANGEMENT

2   How many examples of the present continuous did you hear? Which of the following uses does each example have? To describe:

1   a temporary situation   1 2 3

2   a future arrangement.   4 5

▶ Grammar reference 2.2–2.3 p. 137

3   Complete these sentences with one of the verbs in the box in the correct form of the present continuous.

get	watch	look	speak
go	have	work	rain

1   I 'm.. ..having.. dinner with friends tonight but I'm free at the weekend.

2   ..are.. you ..going.. to Bev's party tomorrow night?

3   We can play tennis now. It ..isn't.. ..raining.. .... any more.

4   I'm not sure where Gavin is. I think he ..is.. ..watching.. TV in the living room.

5   When ..are.. Julie and Simon ..getting.. married?

6   I 'm.. ..not.. ..working.. for the same company any more. I got a new job in October.

7   You ..are.. ..speaking.. much more fluently than when you arrived in England last year.

8   Why ..is.. Petra ..looking.. out of the window? What's happened?

4 Tell another student one thing that you are (probably) doing tonight, next weekend and next holiday.

Example: *Tonight, I'm going bowling with some friends.*

5 Read the text below. There are five mistakes with the present simple or present continuous. Find them and correct them.

All Change!

Everything's changing this week because it's National Break-Your-Routine Week. The idea is that everybody changes at least one thing about their daily routine. It can be small or big, sensible or silly! Stewart Marshall has been out talking to people about how they are changing their routines.

Sally My dad usually drives me to the station and then I'm taking the train to school. But this week I'm walking to the station. I need the exercise!

Keith I eat a bar of chocolate nearly every day, but this week I'm not having any. Maybe I'll stop completely ... I hope so!

Ruth I usually wear black most of the time. So this week I'm trying lots of different colours. Today I wear green and blue. My boyfriend says I look good in it.

Jenny It takes me 45 minutes to get to work on the bus and I don't do usually anything, just daydream. But this week I'm taking a book with me to read. It makes the time go very quickly.

Tom I'm doing everything backwards this week. For example, I am always having cereal for breakfast, so I am having it for dinner this week. And I usually sleep from about 11 p.m. to 7 a.m. ... well, this week I am sleeping in the day from about 8 a.m. to 4 p.m. It's really fun. My friends are thinking I'm crazy!

6 Imagine it is National Break-Your-Routine Week. Look at the categories below and tell a partner your new routine for each one.

food   exercise or sports   clothes   sleep
transportation   reading material   music

Example: Food: *I usually have cereal for breakfast, but this week I'm having chocolate for breakfast.*

Writing: informal letter (1)

1 Look at the informal letter in the Writing reference on page 154 and answer these questions.

1 How does the letter begin and end?
2 Where does each paragraph begin?
3 What is the purpose of each paragraph?

2 Now look at the task and student answer below. The letter has not been divided into separate paragraphs. Decide how many paragraphs there should be in the letter and where each one should begin and end.

Task

You have the name and address of an English language student in another country. Write them a short letter in which you

● introduce yourself
● describe your everyday routine
● say what you like doing in your free time.

Write about 100 words.

STUDENT ANSWER

Dear Eva, My name is Marcia. I'm 14 years old. I live in São Paolo, in Brazil, with my parents and two sisters and I'm really looking forward to getting to know you! Let me tell you a little about my everyday life. During term time, I get up at 7 a.m. After breakfast I get the bus to school. After school, I get home about 3 p.m. when I have something to eat before starting my homework! I like doing lots of different things in my free time. I play volleyball and basketball for my school so that takes up a lot of time! Write soon and tell me about you! Best wishes, Marcia

3 Paragraphs often begin with topic sentences which tell you the subject of the paragraph. See Writing reference (Paragraphs) page 149. What are the topic sentences in paragraphs 2 and 3 in Marcia's letter?

4 Now, write your own answer to the task in Exercise 2. Divide your letter into separate paragraphs. Use topic sentences where possible.

▶ Unit test 2: Teacher's Book

Reading 1

1

1 Discuss these questions with a partner.

 1 Which clothes in the photos do you like best? Why?
 2 What colour do you like wearing best? Why?
 3 Do you usually buy clothes (and bags, phone, etc.) in the same colour or lots of different colours? Why?

2 Read paragraph 1 of the article *Winning colours* and discuss the highlighted questions.

2 Now read the whole article quickly and answer the two highlighted questions. (You don't need to understand every word at this stage.)

Winning colours

1 You are getting ready to play a football match and you want to win. What colour should you wear to help you win? You are getting ready to go to an interview and you want to succeed. What colour should you wear to help you succeed? Strange questions, perhaps, but colour could be the key to your success. Read on and find out how.

School and work – black or blue?

2 The most popular colour in Britain is black. Wearing black makes people *feel* more confident, but can often make you *look* reserved. This may be why people sometimes think that British people don't want to make a strong impression. Although black is common in Britain, most people agree that in fact blue is the world's favourite colour. School uniforms and business suits are often blue. Wearing blue will show that you are an efficient and hard-working person.

Sport – red or yellow?

3 Sometimes people mistakenly think that red makes you look strong, assertive and successful. Often, however, you will be seen as aggressive if you choose red clothes. New information now says that yellow, not red, is the colour of winning. Australia and Brazil are both very successful in the sporting world, and the sports kit of both countries is yellow. Strangely enough, athletes who wear yellow glasses during a race can improve their time by up to half a second. Tests show that the yellow colour makes them feel positive and energetic and could be the difference between a medal and no medal.

4 So, next time you have an important event in your life – a race, a match, an exam or an interview – think about your *clothes*. The colour of your clothes can change your life!

3   Look at the statements below. Read the text again to decide if each statement is true or false.

1   Many people in Britain like wearing black.

2   Black makes British people feel sure about themselves.

3   The most universally popular colour is black.

4   Business people often wear blue.

5   Red is a good colour to wear for an interview.

6   Red and yellow are both colours for success.

7   The sports clothes of both Australia and Brazil are yellow.

8   Wearing yellow glasses can make people run faster.

4   Paragraphs 2 and 3 of the text contain some adjectives which describe personality. Look at the following sentences and find a word in paragraphs 2 or 3 to complete each one.

Example: People who are *reserved* don't like talking about their feelings.

1   .... people are sure that they can do things well.

2   An .... person works well, without wasting time or energy.

3   A .... person puts a lot of effort into their work.

4   Someone who is physically powerful is ....

5   If you are ...., you say what you think in a confident way.

6   Someone who is .... behaves angrily.

5   Work with a partner and discuss these questions.

1   Look around the classroom. What is/are the most popular colour(s) that the students are wearing? Why?

2   What colours would you never wear? Why?

3   What colour are the walls of your classroom? Do you like them? Why?/ Why not?

Grammar 1: gerunds

1

1   Look at pictures A and B. Match each example sentence below (1 and 2) with the correct picture. What kind of word is the underlined word in each sentence?

1   <u>Wearing</u> black clothes makes me feel confident.
2   I feel nervous about <u>wearing</u> bright colours.

2   Match the sentences above with the correct rule.

- We use gerunds after **prepositions**.
- We use gerunds when an activity is the **subject** of a sentence.

Watch Out   gerund or infinitive?••••••••

Which alternative is correct in each sentence? Why?

1   It's fun to *go/going* shopping.
2   I'm looking forward to *go/going* to the party.
3   I'd like to *go/going* to the party.

▶ Grammar reference 3.1 p. 138

2   Underline all the gerunds after prepositions and circle all the gerunds used as subjects.

Example: (Swimming) is a good way **of** <u>getting</u> fit.

1   I told my best friend the news before telling everyone else.

2   Being afraid of flying means I usually go on holiday in this country.

3   Living with other people is often quite difficult.

4   He's using it for keeping old newspapers in.

5   I'm looking forward to hearing from you.

3   Rewrite the sentences using gerunds as subjects.

Example: It is very relaxing to listen to music.
Listening to music is very relaxing.

1 It is difficult to speak another language well.

2 It isn't healthy to eat a lot of fat and sugar.

3 It is important to write clearly in an exam.

4 One of my favourite things is to go shopping.

5 It's cheaper to get a video than to go to the cinema.

6 It's a good idea to talk about things that worry you.

7 It's illegal to drive a car when you're 15.

8 Do you think it's a waste of money to buy CDs?

4   Complete the sentences by choosing the correct verb from the box and deciding if it is a gerund or not.

Example: *He's really worried about **flying** to Australia.*

arrive	cook	~~fly~~
get	give	play
see	use	wait

1 I'm tired of .... for Alex – he's half an hour late!

2 She's not interested in .... ball games.

3 I really don't know how to .... this computer properly.

4 They are thinking about .... tickets for the show next week.

5 My brother is really good at .... French food.

6 I'm looking forward to .... you soon.

7 I can't decide what to .... Kim for her birthday.

8 They apologised for .... late.

5   Complete the sentences below to make them true for you. Compare and discuss your sentences with a partner.

1 I'm really interested in ....

2 I'm looking forward to ....

3 .... is something that makes me nervous.

4 .... is one of my favourite things to do at the weekend.

Vocabulary: word formation

1   *Suffixes* are letters that you can add to the end of a word. A suffix can change the meaning of the word and the kind of word it is (noun, verb, adjective, etc.). Look at the underlined words in the examples below. What kind of word is each one (noun, verb or adjective)?

1 Painting the room white will really improve it.   ....

2 Painting the room white will be a real improvement.   ....

3 Being lazy is my only weak point.   ....

4 Being lazy is my only weakness.   ....

2   Complete the table below. If you are unsure of the spellings or the meanings of any of the words, check in a good English–English dictionary (e.g. *Longman Wordwise Dictionary*).

From **verb** to **noun**, use the suffixes:	-ment improve – *improvement* excite – .... enjoy –	-ion/-tion/-ation inform – .... impress – .... reduce – ....
From **adjective** to **noun**, use the suffixes:	-ness weak – *weakness* lazy –	-ity secure – .... flexible – ....

3   For each question, complete the second sentence with one word so that it means the same as the first.

Example: I only feel secure when I wear black.
    Wearing black gives me a feeling of *security.*

1 I want to improve my clothes and hair.
   I want to make some .... to my clothes and hair.

2 The price of these jeans was reduced from £60 to £40.
   There was a £20 .... in the price of these jeans.

3 We need to inform you about what clothes to wear.
   We need to give you important .... about what clothes to wear.

4 We are very flexible about what kind of clothes
you wear.
There is a lot of .... about what kind of clothes
you wear.

5 Lots of people got very excited about the film star's
new dress.
A lot of .... was caused by the film star's
new dress.

Speaking

1

1 Look at the photos opposite and complete the
example sentences in the speech bubbles.

⚡ When you talk about a photograph, it is useful to be able to
organise what you are going to say. You can start by talking
in a general way.

First, summarise the content of the photograph.

A

*This photo shows a busy market with
people selling fruit and vegetables.*

B

This photo shows ....

Then, say where you think the photo was taken
and why.

A

I think it was taken ....

B

*I think it was taken in an English-speaking
country because the magazines have
English on them. It could be in the USA,
but I'm not sure.*

2 You can then talk about the details in the picture.
Look at the sentences below. Which picture does
each one refer to?

1 She looks quite friendly.
2 It looks like quite a boring job.
3 He looks as if he can't decide what to buy.
4 It looks as if you can pay by credit card.

2

1 We can use the verb *to look* in different
ways to describe a picture. Complete the
sentences below with *like*, *as if* or nothing.
Use the examples above to help you.

1 He looks .... friendly.
2 He looks .... a friendly person.
3 He looks .... he's a friendly person.

2 Write three more sentences for the pictures
using the verb *to look*.

3   Work with a partner and take it in turns
to describe one picture. Use the phrases in
Exercises 1 and 2 to help you.

Listening 1

1   Think of a smell you like and a smell you hate. Tell a partner.

2   You will hear some people talking about things you smell. Listen to the extracts and answer this question.

In which of the extracts are the people a) positive, b) negative, c) neutral?

3   Listen again and put a tick (✓) under the correct pictures.

A   B   C

1   Which situation is the woman talking about?

A   B   C

3   Which does the man say is the biggest problem for him?

A   B   C

4   What new products with added smells does the woman say you can buy?

A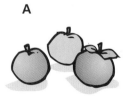   B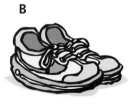   C

5   How much does the perfume cost?

A £4,750   B £47,750   C £74,750

Reading 2: labels

1   Do not spray in or around the eyes

1

1   Look at the label on the bottle of perfume above and read the words. On what other things might you see a similar label?

2   To get a general idea of what the following labels are saying, read them quickly and answer the questions below.

⚡ It can help to look at the style of the labels as well as the words.

2   ⚠ This contains dangerous chemicals.

3   ✚ If swallowed, get a doctor immediately.

4 | May make you sleepy. If affected, do not drive.

5   Keep out of the reach of children

6   In case of contact with eyes, wash with water.

1   Where would you see these labels? Choose two of the following.
   a) on bottles of medicine
   b) on packets of food
   c) on office equipment
   d) on cleaning products

2   Generally, which of the following are they concerned with?
   a) explaining how to use the product
   b) warning about possible dangers
   c) telling you how to open it

2   Now, look again at each label. Someone asks you what it means. Choose the correct explanation – A, B or C.

1 A This is safe to put in your eyes. ☐
   B It's not a good idea to use this near your eyes. ☑
   C Only use this for eyes. ☐

2 A These chemicals may harm or kill you. ☐
   B These chemicals are safe to drink. ☐
   C No dangerous chemicals should be put in this. ☐

3 A Get a doctor quickly if you have problems swallowing this. ☐
   B Eat this as soon as you've seen your doctor. ☐
   C Get a doctor quickly if you eat this. ☐

4 A This won't make you feel sleepy when you're driving your car. ☐
   B If you feel sleepy after taking this medicine, don't use your car. ☐
   C Don't drive your car until you feel sleepy. ☐

5 A Put this in a place where children can't get it. ☐
   B Children should be able to reach this easily. ☐
   C Keep this until children need it. ☐

6 A This is safe to use, if you put water in your eyes first. ☐
   B Put water on your contact lenses before putting them in your eyes. ☐
   C You need to wash this out with water if it goes in your eyes. ☐

3 Do you know what to do in these medical emergency situations? Discuss what you should do with another student.

1 Someone gets dangerous chemicals in their eyes.
2 You find a child with an empty medicine bottle.
3 Someone stops breathing.
4 Someone gets burned.

Grammar 2: gerunds and infinitives

1   Some verbs are always followed by a gerund and some are always followed by an infinitive. Look at the sentences below and complete the rules (A and B) by writing *gerund* or *infinitive*.

1 I **enjoy** *shopping* in street markets.
2 Can you **imagine** *being* allergic to perfume?
3 I **decided** *to sit* at the back of the restaurant.

A
- The verbs *enjoy* and *imagine* are always followed by the ....
- Other verbs that follow this rule are:
  avoid   consider   finish   involve   suggest

B
- The verbs *decide* and *plan* are always followed by the ....
- Other verbs that follow this rule are:
  agree   arrange   hope   manage   offer

4 She is **planning** *to have* a party.

▶ Grammar reference 3.2 p. 138

2   Choose the correct alternative after each highlighted verb in the letter below.

Dear Auntie Jean,
   It's my birthday soon and some friends have suggested (1) having/to have a big party. I know I won't be able to avoid (2) doing/to do a lot of work before the day. Parties always involve (3) doing/to do much more preparation than you think! Mum and Dad have agreed (4) helping/to help with the preparations. I considered (5) using/to use a professional caterer for the food, but it was too expensive. So, Mum has offered (6) making/to make the food.
   I haven't decided what to wear yet, but I've arranged (7) going/to go shopping with a friend tomorrow. I'm hoping (8) finding/to find something to go with some great shoes I've got.
   I'm sure we'll manage (9) finishing/to finish everything if everyone helps. First, I need to finish (10) doing/to do the invitations - but there are already 75 people on the list and I know I've forgotten some people! I'll write again and tell you all about how it went.
Lots of love,
Carina

3   Complete the second sentence so that it is similar in meaning to the first sentence.

Example: I did all my work yesterday.

I finished _doing all my work yesterday._

1   I'll help her with the shopping.
I offered ....
....

2   I'd like to buy some shoes today.
I'm hoping ....
....

3   OK, I'll go with him.
I agreed ....
....

4   I think I might ask Jessica to help me.
I'm considering ....
....

5   We finally finished the project!
We finally managed ....
....

6   Let's go to the cinema.
I suggested ....
....

7   I don't want to see Manuel.
I want to avoid ....
....

8   We're going to walk a lot on holiday.
The holiday involves ....
....

9   OK, I'll meet you at 6 o'clock.
We arranged ....
....

10   There isn't any more cooking to do.
I've finished ....
....

Listening 2: song

1   You're going to listen to a song by The Corrs. Before you listen, look at the pictures and imagine a story to link them. Compare your story with a partner's.

2   Listen to the song and write the letters of the pictures in the order you hear them.

Example: *Picture B, …*

I've (0) .....seen........ this place a thousand times
I've (1) .... this all before
And every time you call
I've waited there as though you might not call at all
I know this face I'm wearing now
I've (2) .... this with my eyes
And though it (3) .... so great I'm still afraid
That you'll be leaving anytime
We've done this once and then you closed the door
Don't let me fall again for nothing more
Don't (4) .... you love me unless forever
Don't tell me you need me if you're not gonna stay
Don't give me this (5) .... I'll only believe it
Make it real or take it all away
I've caught myself smiling alone
Just thinking of your (6) ....
And dreaming of your (7) .... is all too much
You know I don't have any choice

3   Look at the words related to the senses in the box. Before you listen again, put them in the correct place in the song. Then listen and check.

| say | ~~seen~~ | seen | touch |
| voice | feeling | feels | felt |

4   Listen again and answer the questions.

1   Does she think he'll phone her or not?

2   Is it the first time she's felt like this?

3   Why is she afraid?

4   Why does she say 'Don't say you love me'?

5   Does she think about hearing him or seeing him?

A

B

C

D

Writing: informal letter (2)

1

1 Look at the task below. What film or play could you write about? How many words should you write?

Task

You've seen a very good film or play recently. Now you are writing a letter to an English-speaking friend to tell him or her all about it. Say what film (or play) you saw, what it was about and why you enjoyed it so much.

Write 100–120 words.

2 Read Danka's letter to her friend Marianne and answer the questions.

1 What film has she seen?
2 Does she tell her the ending of the film? Why?/Why not?

> Dear Marianne
> 1 Thanks for your last letter. It was good to hear from you.
> 2 I'm writeing to tell you about a really good film I've seen recently, called Chocolat. The main star of the film is Juliette Binoche. She plays a woman who goes to live in a small French town and opens a chocolate shop. Strange things start happening, and the people in the town get angryer and angryer. I won't tell you any more because you should go and see it yourself!
> 3 It is an unusual plot and a beautiful film. The acting is very good, too. I'm planing to go to the cinema again tonight!
> Love
> Danka

2 Read the letter again and match the descriptions below (a–c) to the paragraph numbers.

a) describing the film ....
b) general opinion about the film ....
c) referring to friend's last letter ....

3

1 Read the letter again and find words that mean the same as each definition below.

1 *n* the most important actor in a film or play: ....
2 *v* to take part in a play or film as one of the characters: ....
3 *n* the main events in a film, play or book: ....
4 *n* the way of performing in a film or play: ....

2 There are three spelling mistakes in Danka's letter. Find the words and write the correct spelling for each type of mistake below.

1 Words ending in *-e*, (or *-ee* or *-ie*).
2 Words ending in *-y*.
3 One-syllable words ending in one vowel and one consonant.

▶ Writing reference (Spelling) p. 151

4   You are going to do the task in Exercise 1.

1 Choose one of the films in the photos or choose a good film (or play) you've seen recently. Tell your partner about it. What was it about? Why did you like it?

2 What vocabulary will you need to write about the film (or play)? Write down three words or phrases that you think will be useful. You can also use the words in Exercise 3 if necessary.

5   Decide how many paragraphs your letter will have. What will the subject of each one be? (Refer to Exercise 2.) Make notes for each paragraph.

▶ Writing reference (Paragraphs) p. 149

6   Write your letter (100–120 words). Check that the layout and the start and finish are appropriate for an informal letter.

▶ Writing reference (Informal letters) p. 154

▶ Progress test 1: Teacher's Book

1   Match these questions and answers.

1 What's your first name?
2 How do you spell your surname?
3 What do you do?
4 How long have you been living in England?
5 Why are you learning English?
6 Whose bag is that?
7 How many times have you been to the cinema this year?
8 When did you last see your grandparents?
9 How often do you do some exercise?
10 Where were you born?
11 How much does it cost to fly to Poland?
12 Who is your favourite sportsperson?

a) I'm an engineer.
b) I try to go to the gym twice a week.
c) Tiger Woods. He's an incredible golfer.
d) In Thessaloniki, in the north of Greece.
e) Helen's. She asked me to look after it.
f) About £200.
g) To help me get a better job.
h) Nearly a year.
i) About a month ago. I'm going to visit them next weekend.
j) Lots! I go as often as I can.
k) Anna.
l) D-E-A-C-O-N.

2   Decide if the verbs in these sentences are in the correct tense or not. If not, correct them.

1 I am usually having cereal and toast for breakfast.

....

2 He's playing football in the garden right now.

....

3 She visits her sister in Australia next week.

....

4 I am not knowing what time the match starts.

....

5 First you go to the administration office to find out which class you are in.

....

6 He lives in Warsaw where he was brought up.

....

7 They travel around Italy at the moment.

....

8 I stay with some friends for a few days until I find my own place.

....

3   Change these direct questions into indirect questions. Begin with the words given.

1 a) How much is that jacket?
   Could you ....
  b) Do you have this jacket in other colours?
   I'd also like to ....

2 a) What time does the film start?
   Could you ....
  b) How long does the film last?
   I'd also like to ....

3 a) Do you have any English–English dictionaries?
   Could you ....
  b) How much is this grammar book?
   I'd also like to ....

4 a) How do you get to the nearest post office?
   Could you ....
  b) How far is it from here?
   I'd also like to ....

4   Decide if the following sentences are correctly punctuated or not. If not, correct the mistakes.

1 she bought two pairs of jeans six T-shirts some shoes and a black jacket.

....

2 I'm going to have lunch with Peter in Cambridge on Thursday.

....

3 We drove to paris found a hotel and then had a fantastic meal in a local restaurant.

....

4 Ive left my keys in Johns car.

....

5 If I see harriet I'll tell her you want to talk to her.

....

5 Unjumble the words (connected with *family, free time activities* and *senses*) in these sentences.

1 My *otrerdnamgh* is going to be ninety-two next birthday. ....

2 My brother is much older than me, so my *sceeni* are nearly my age! ....

3 I see a lot of my *nucssoi*. Our parents never moved away from where they were brought up. ....

4 My *ptfrseehta* has two children by his previous marriage but they've left home now. ....

5 My parents bought me a new camera and I'm taking lots of *oopphhstarg* with it. ....

6 My granddad is really good at *ssehc* but he usually lets me win! ....

7 I go *gggnijo* with my friend, Laura, every morning. We usually run about three miles. ....

8 He's been playing the *raugit* for years and he occasionally plays in a band. ....

9 I love the *lemsl* of fresh coffee! ....

10 Don't *uthco* the plate. It's very hot. ....

11 She heard a *iseon* and went downstairs to investigate. ....

12 Can you *esatt* the sauce and tell me if you like it? ....

6 Use the word given in capitals at the end of each sentence to form a word that fits in the space.

1 Shall I send you some .... about our language courses? **INFORM**

2 Sending her flowers was a sign of real .... **THOUGHT**

3 He never believed he would know such .... **HAPPY**

4 We hope the bad weather didn't spoil your .... **ENJOY**

5 You must find an .... way of organising your work. **EFFICIENCY**

6 He's in charge of .... at the airport. **SECURE**

7 My father became quite .... when I was given a prize at school. **EMOTION**

8 The trees gave them some .... against the rain. **PROTECT**

7 Make the verbs in brackets gerunds or infinitives as appropriate.

1 I really enjoy .... (*visit*) places I've never been to before.

2 We've decided .... (*move*) to Scotland.

3 Have you finished .... (*watch*) TV?

4 He agreed .... (*tidy*) up his room before he went out.

5 She's hoping .... (*live*) in Mexico for a few months and learn Spanish.

6 I'm considering .... (*apply*) for a new job.

7 Sylvia suggested .... (*go*) swimming as it was such a nice day.

8 He offered .... (*teach*) her how to play the piano.

8 Look at this extract from a story. Try to work out the approximate meaning of the eight underlined words from their contexts.

In the moonlight, Sophie caught a <u>glimpse</u> of an enormous long pale <u>wrinkly</u> face with the most enormous ears. The nose was as <u>sharp</u> as a knife, and above the nose there were two bright <u>flashing</u> eyes, and the eyes were <u>staring</u> straight at Sophie. Sophie gave a <u>yelp</u> and pulled back from the window. She flew across the dormitory and jumped into her bed and hid under the blanket. And there she <u>crouched</u>, still as a mouse, and <u>tingling</u> all over.

4 Practice makes perfect?

Reading

1 Look at the photographs and the words in the box. Check with a partner if you are not sure of the meanings of any of the words.

> a cello   a nightclub DJ
> record decks
> to mix records

2

⚡ You will find it easier to understand a text if you predict the content before you read. You can predict the content of a text from the title and any pictures.

Discuss these questions with a partner.

1 Look again at the photos of Sian. What do they tell you about her?

2 The title of the text is *Faking it*. Read the dictionary definition below. What does the title tell you about the content of the text?

> **fake (it)** /feɪk/ v to pretend to be something that you are not

3 Read the text quickly. Were your answers to the questions in Exercise 2 correct?

Faking it

Sian Evans is 22. Until last year, she lived a quiet life, playing the cello and studying music at university. Then one day, she was given a challenge. She agreed to take part in a television programme called *Faking it*. She had just four weeks to learn completely new skills and become a nightclub DJ. At the end of her training, she had to perform and compete against three professional DJs. She had to convince the judges that she wasn't a fake.

For a month, Sian stayed with top DJ, Anne. When Sian first met her, she felt totally out of place. She said, 'She is so glamorous. I was really quite scared at first.' Almost as soon as she arrived, however, Sian started her training. She had lessons in 'mixing' the music on Anne's record decks. She had voice training to make her sound right: 'I learned to shout with attitude!' said Sian. To make her look right, she had new clothes, a new haircut and even dancing lessons. It wasn't only lessons, however. She also practised. She practised everything, but mostly the 'mixing'. She was on the decks for at least five hours a day.

At the end of the month, Sian and three other professional DJs performed in front of the judges. Their job was to pick the 'fake'. None of them picked Sian. In fact, they couldn't believe it when they were told. She was professional and confident, due mostly to enormous amounts of dedicated practice. Immediately after the programme, she was offered a job as a professional DJ in a top nightclub. So, perhaps it's true that 'practice makes perfect'!

4   Read the text again and for each question, choose the correct answer – A, B or C.

1 What was Sian doing before last year?
   A She was hoping to go to university. ☐
   B She was studying at university. ☑
   C She was teaching at university. ☐

2 What challenge was she given?
   A to make a television programme about a professional DJ ☐
   B to learn to be a professional DJ ☐
   C to teach a professional DJ to play the cello ☐

3 How did Sian feel when she first met Anne?
   A nervous ☐
   B confident ☐
   C excited ☐

4 Why did Sian have voice training?
   A to learn to sing in a nightclub ☐
   B to learn to speak more loudly ☐
   C to learn to speak more quietly ☐

5 What did the judges think of Sian?
   A They thought she needed more practice. ☐
   B They thought she was the 'fake'. ☐
   C They didn't believe she learned in only a month. ☐

6 What happened after the programme?
   A She got the chance to take a job as a DJ. ☐
   B She applied for a job as a DJ. ☐
   C She rejected a job as a DJ. ☐

5   Discuss these questions with other students.

1 What does 'practice makes perfect' mean?

2 Do you think that people who do well are usually born that way or do you think that 'practice makes perfect'?

3 Do you think you could do what Sian did in one month? Why?/Why not?

Grammar 1: past simple/continuous

1

1 Match each sentence (1–3) with the correct rule (a–c).
   1 I **went** to a really good nightclub last weekend.
   2 While I **was studying**, my sister **was watching** a video.

   a) Past continuous: two (or more) past actions happening at the same time
   b) Past continuous: a continuous action interrupted by a finished action (in the past simple)
   c) Past simple: a finished action or situation in the past

   3 I **was practising** the guitar when my friend **arrived**.

2 Which of the following sentences are incorrect? Why?
   1 I was practising the guitar *when* my friend arrived.
   2 I was practising the guitar *while* my friend arrived.
   3 *When* I was studying for my exam, my sister was watching a video.
   4 *While* I was studying for my exam, my sister was watching a video.

▶ Grammar reference 4.1 p. 138

2   Complete the sentences with your own ideas. Use the past continuous.

Example: I cut my finger while I *was cooking dinner.* ....

1 Thomas fell asleep while he ....

2 Their car broke down while they ....

3 While I was having breakfast, my brother ....

4 The phone rang while I ....

5 Fiona fell over while she ....

6 While I was sending him an email, he ....

3   Write the verbs in brackets in the correct form, past simple or past continuous.

Example: I *was watching* (watch) a video when Sam *arrived* (arrive).

1 While I .... (live) in Australia, I .... (go) to the Sydney Olympics.

2 She .... (start) learning French six years ago.

3 While I .... (tidy) the house, my brothers .... (play) football.

4 Sara .... (not look) at the road when someone .... (walk) out in front of her car.

5 He .... (not study) very hard for his exams and he .... (not pass) any of them.

6 My mother .... (cut) her finger while she .... (cook) dinner.

4   Complete the email message below using the correct form of the verbs in the box. Use the past simple and past continuous.

break	cycle	fall	get
~~have~~	start	run	talk
go	try	wait	

Dear Costas,

Last week I (1) ...*had*.......... a lot of bad luck while I (2) .... to and from school. On Monday, I (3) .... for 35 minutes for a bus! Then while I (4) .... to read my book on the bus, three people (5) .... really loudly on their mobile phones. On Wednesday, I decided to walk, but it (6) .... raining and I (7) .... completely soaked. On Friday, I (8) .... to school when a dog suddenly (9) .... out in front of my bicycle. I (10) .... off and (11) .... my arm! So I can't play basketball with you tomorrow. I'll phone you later.

Dimitri

5

1   Answer the questions below by guessing. (Don't ask your partner yet.)

1   What do you think your partner did last weekend?
2   What do you think your partner did before breakfast this morning?
3   What do you think your partner was doing at 7 o'clock last night?
4   What do you think your partner was doing at lunchtime yesterday?
5   What do you think your partner was thinking about while he or she was coming to school?

2   Now ask your partner. How many answers did you guess correctly?

Listening

1   Look at the pictures and discuss these questions with a partner.

1   Why do people do the things in the pictures? Choose reasons from the box (or give any others you can think of).

for fun   to pass the time   to exercise their brains
to improve their memories   to get a better job

2   Do you do any of these things? Why?/Why not?

2   Listen to Daniel and Maria talking about improving your brainpower. Are they both sure it is possible to become more intelligent?

3

1   You're going to listen again and answer more detailed questions. First, read the statements below and try to decide if they are true or false.

⚡ Reading the questions before you listen will help you to listen for the information you need.

1   Maria has heard about 'neurobics' before. *false*....
2   Daniel thinks that it's good to do mental exercise. ....
3   Maria thought that your brain only developed until the age of twelve. ....
4   The magazine says that hard work is necessary to increase intelligence. ....
5   Daniel says that exercising reduces the amount of oxygen going to the brain. ....
6   Daniel says that learning languages is good mental exercise. ....
7   Maria wants a bigger brain. ....

2   Now listen again and decide if each statement is true or false.

4   Try these mind games with a partner.

1 Draw this shape without taking your pencil off the paper or going over the same line twice.

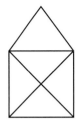

2 What's the next number in this sequence?
1 4 10 19 31 ....

3 How many words can you make from the word *education*?

Example: *tie*

Do you know any other mind games?

Vocabulary 1: education

1   You can get a lot of information about words from a good English–English dictionary, like the *Longman Wordwise Dictionary*. Look at the dictionary entry below for the word *timetable*. Answer the questions with a partner.

1 What part of speech is *timetable*?

2 How many syllables does *timetable* have?

3 Where is the main stress on *timetable*?

4 Does the dictionary show you how to pronounce *timetable*?

5 What example does the dictionary give you?

6 Is the definition of *timetable* helpful?

how many syllables

main stress

spelling

pronunciation

time•ta•ble /'taɪm,teɪbəl/ *noun* a list of times or dates, showing when things will happen: *the train timetable*

definition

example in context

part of speech (e.g. *noun, verb, adjective,* etc.)

2   Here are some questions that you might ask someone from Britain. Look at the words in italics. Use an English–English dictionary to help you check:

a) the meaning,

b) the part of speech, and

c) the pronunciation.

1 Is the *timetable* at school the same every day?

2 Do all children go to *nursery school*?

3 What age do you go to *primary school*?

4 What age do you go to *secondary school*?

5 Does everyone *leave school* at 16?

6 What age do teenagers *take public exams*?

7 How long does *a degree course* usually last?

8 When do you do a *postgraduate course*?

9 How many *terms* are there in the *academic year*?

10 What *subjects* can you do at *university*?

3   Match the questions (1–10) in Exercise 2 with the answers (A–J) below about the education system in Britain.

Example: *1–B*

A 16 and 18.

B No, you do different things.

C You have to go between the ages of 11 and 16.

D Three years.

E No, some people stay at school until they're 18.

F I did business studies, but you can study lots of different things.

G You have to go between the ages of 5 and 11.

H After you've got your first degree.

I Three: September to December; January to March; April to July.

J No, only some go between the ages of 3 and 4.

4   Work with a partner and describe the education system in your country using the questions in Exercise 2 to help you.

Example: *In my country, not many children go to nursery school. I didn't start primary school until I was six.*

Speaking

1

A

B

⚡ Try to use information in a photo to guess or speculate about what is happening.

1 These sentences are speculating about photo A. Which do you think are true and which are false? Change the false sentences to make them true.

1 *It looks like* a chemistry lesson.
2 *They might be* about 16.
3 *It seems to be* a boys' school.
4 *It's probably* a very interesting lesson.
5 *They look as if* they are very bored.
6 *It seems as if* they're doing an experiment.

2 These sentences speculate about photo B. Complete each sentence with one word.

1 *It seems* .... *be* a school trip.
2 *They look* .... *if* they are in the country.
3 *They* .... *be* about nine or ten.
4 *It seems as* .... they're enjoying themselves.
5 *It* .... *probably* in Britain.
6 *It* .... *like* a fun lesson.

2

⚡ If you organise what you say, it will make it easier for people to listen to.

1 Look at the first three stages of the description (1–3) and match them with the correct example sentences (A–C).

1 First summarise the content of the photograph.
2 Then say where you think the photo was taken and why.
3 Then talk about some details, e.g. speculate about what is happening.

A *I think it was taken in a secondary school in Britain because of the clothes they are wearing.*
B *The boys look as if they are very bored.*
C *This photo shows a class of teenage boys at school.*

2 Work with a partner and choose one photo each. Take it in turns to talk about your photo. Follow the stages above and try to use the phrases from Exercise 1.

3 Discuss the following questions with a partner.

1 Do you think school trips (e.g. to the zoo, museums, etc.) are a useful way of learning? Why?/Why not?
2 What subjects do you think are the most important to study at school? Why?
3 Do intelligent people always do well at school? Why?/Why not?
4 Do you think that a good education should prepare you for life in general or for a particular job? Why?

Use of English: cloze

1   Discuss these questions with a partner.

1 How many different languages can you speak?

2 When and where did you start learning them?

2   You are going to read a text about learning languages. To help you get the general idea, read the text quickly and say which of the following (a–c) summarises the general idea best.

a) The school only teaches languages.

b) The school has very good language teachers.

c) The school teaches different subjects in different languages.

Last week *Unity International School* (1) _celebrated_ their tenth anniversary. They held an open day for visitors to see their unique school.

When I arrived, I immediately (2) .... how confident the students were. What was different from other schools, however, was how they talked to (3) .... other. I heard students (4) .... in English, French, Spanish and German. They were completely at (5) .... with these languages and changed from one to (6) .... without thinking. This is because languages are not *what* they study, but *how* they study. They study history in Spanish, maths in German and (7) .... on. Anna, a 14-year-old student, (8) .... me, 'I came here two years ago. Before that I had never learned any foreign languages. Now I am (9) .... in four languages. I feel very lucky.'

Go and see (10) .... yourself. This is an amazing and special school. I (11) .... them every success for another ten years and more!

3   For each question below, circle the letter next to the correct word – A, B, C or D. To help you decide on the correct word, read the whole sentence, especially the words before and after the space.

1 A welcomed   B remembered   C celebrated   D performed
2 A meant   B reminded   C watched   D noticed
3 A every   B each   C one   D all
4 A saying   B speaking   C pronouncing   D translating
5 A ease   B comfortable   C confident   D happy
6 A all   B one   C other   D another
7 A more   B further   C later   D so
8 A talked   B told   C said   D spoke
9 A fluid   B fluidly   C fluent   D fluently
10 A by   B for   C with   D at
11 A wish   B want   C make   D do

4   Discuss the questions with a partner.

1 What do you think would be the best and worst things about *Unity International School*?

2 Would you like to go to a school like this? Why?/Why not?

Grammar 2: past perfect

1   Look at the underlined verbs in the sentence below. Complete the rules (A and B) by deciding if the action happened first or second.

I <u>had</u> <u>studied</u> Spanish for two years before I <u>came</u> to this school.

A

We use the past perfect simple (e.g. *had studied*) because the action happened *first/second*.

B

We use the past simple (e.g. *came*) because the action happened *first/second*.

► Grammar reference 4.2 p.138

2   In each sentence below, write 1 next to the action which happened first, and write 2 next to the action which happened second.

Example: *By the time I saw Silvia again*
                                    2
she had married John.
                1

1 After I'd finished my essay, I went to the gym.

2 Bettina phoned me as soon as her plane had landed.

3 When he'd spoken to Janice, he left.

4 As soon as Simone had finished her dinner, she went to bed.

5 I tried to phone Angela, but she'd gone out.

6 By the time we arrived at the party, everyone had gone.

3   Complete these sentences using the verbs in brackets. Use the past simple or the past perfect simple.

Example: The bus was late, so when we ...*arrived*.... (*arrive*) the film *had started*.. (*start*).

1 As soon as we .... (*bring*) everything inside, the sun .... (*come*) out.

2 I realised I .... (*meet*) Pedro before, the moment I .... (*see*) him.

3 He .... (*feel*) nervous because he .... (*not fly*) in a plane before.

4 I remembered that I .... (*see*) the film before as soon as it .... (*start*).

5 When she .... (*arrive*) at the supermarket, it .... (*close*).

6 When I .... (*see*) the pizza, I remembered that I .... (*not eat*) all day.

4

1 Match the beginnings (1–5) with the ends (a–e) to make appropriate sentences.

Beginnings	Ends
1 By the time I got to the pet shop,	a) we still had no idea where he was.
2 As soon as she left,	b) it had completely disappeared.
3 So, after we had spent the whole day looking,	c) he'd already bought and paid for a huge black snake.
4 When everyone arrived to see what I had found in the forest,	d) he had thrown it away.
5 Before I was able to tell my brother about the lottery ticket,	e) I realised I had made the biggest mistake of my life.

2 Work with a partner and choose one of the sentences. Say what you think happened before and after the sentence you've chosen.

Vocabulary 2: adverbs of manner

1

1 Complete the labels on sentences 1 and 2. Write *adjective*, *adverb*, *noun* or *verb*.

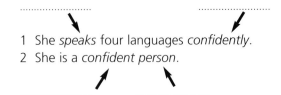

1 She *speaks* four languages *confidently*.
2 She is a *confident person*.

2 Complete the rules below (A and B) by writing *adjectives* or *adverbs*.

A

We use .... to tell us about **verbs**. They tell us how somebody does something or how something happens. They come after the verb in a sentence.

B

We use .... to tell us about **nouns**. They come before the noun in a sentence.

2   Complete each sentence with the correct word in brackets (adverb or adjective).

Example: My brother usually drives very ...*carefully*... . (*careful/carefully*)

1 She is a very .... driver. (*careful/carefully*)

2 They lived .... together for many years. (*happy/happily*)

3 He walked .... into the exam room. (*nervous/nervously*)

4 She's a really .... person and she doesn't often smile. (*serious/seriously*)

5 My neighbours were shouting .... (*loud/loudly*)

6 He speaks so .... that I can't hear him. (*quiet/quietly*)

3

1 For each of the situations in the box, think about when you did or usually do these things and why.

Examples: *I usually get dressed quickly in the mornings because I get up too late.*

get dressed quickly	shout loudly	work hard
sleep badly	read carefully	play well

2 Tell your partner about each situation, giving your reasons.

Writing: story (2)

1 You are going to read a story about the picture above. The title of the story is *A little practice can be dangerous!* Before you read, look at the picture and the title. Tell another student what you think the story is about.

2 The story has three paragraphs. Decide the correct order of sentences for each paragraph. The first paragraph has been done for you.

Paragraph 1

4 A They decided to go further and soon they were in the middle of the river.

2 B 'Let's have a go,' said Jon.

3 C At first, it was difficult but with a little practice, they became more confident.

1 D One afternoon, Marek and Jon were walking along the river when they saw a rowing boat.

Paragraph 2

E To get there, however, they had to row against the water.

F They weren't strong enough and the boat went faster and faster in the wrong direction.

G After a while, they decided to go back to the riverbank.

Paragraph 3

H Marek and Jon went home. They knew they had been stupid and were lucky to be alive.

I The boys shouted for help but nobody heard them.

J Finally, a man in a large motorboat saw them and helped them to safety.

3 Look again at the first sentence of the story in Exercise 2 and answer the questions below.

1 What tells you it is the first sentence?

2 Why is it better than these first sentences?
Marek and Jon had finished school.
They were walking along the river on their way home from school.

▶ Writing reference (Making your writing interesting) p. 150

4

1 Find five time expressions in five of the sentences in Exercise 2.

Example: *One afternoon*, Marek and Jon were walking along the river when they saw a rowing boat.

2 Choose the correct time expression for each of the sentences below.

1 He opened the map and looked at it. *At first/ Finally* he didn't know where to go, but then it became clear.

2 Harry was waiting at a bus stop. *One afternoon/ After a while* he realised that he couldn't see anybody else around.

3 She had spent the whole day waiting for Sindy to arrive. It was late. *Finally/Soon* she decided to go home.

4 *At first/One afternoon*, James was getting ready to go out skating with some friends.

5 They started walking up the mountain but at *first/ soon* they felt very tired.

5 You are going to write a story with the title *A little practice can be dangerous!* Before you write your story, follow these preparation stages.

1 Write down any **ideas** you have for your story.

2 Tick the ideas that you think are the **best** ones.

3 Divide your ideas into three paragraphs:

A setting the scene

B main events of the story

C what happens in the end

6 Now write your story (about 100 words).

▶ Unit test 4: Teacher's Book

UNIT
5 Behind the mask

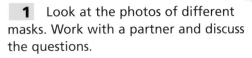

1 Look at the photos of different masks. Work with a partner and discuss the questions.

1 What part of the world do you think each one comes from?

2 Which one do you like best? Why?

2

⚡ When somebody gives a talk, they usually give a short introduction. They say what they are going to talk about in a general way first. This can help the audience predict the rest of the talk.

📻 1 Listen to the introduction of a talk on the radio. What do you think the rest of the talk will be about?

2 Now discuss your predictions with a partner.

📻 3 Look at the list of different uses for masks below. Listen to the whole talk and number the different uses in the order they are mentioned.

curing illness ☐
dressing up for parties ☐
helping farmers grow food ☐
representing characters in drama ☐
remembering people from the past ☐

3

1 Look at the notes below about the *Masks of the world* exhibition. What kind of information is missing in each space (e.g. year, country, etc.)?

Exhibition: *Masks of the world*

Masks for the dead – country: Egypt
Tutankhamun's mask made in (1) .... BC

Masks of the 'shaman' or (2) .... man – country: Indonesia

'Food-growing' masks – country: (3) ....

Rain and clouds are on masks worn by (4) ....

Masks for parties and festivals e.g. Hallowe'en and (5) ....

Masks in the theatre – countries: (6) .... and Japan

---

📻 2 Listen again and for each question, fill in the missing information in the numbered space.

4 Discuss these questions with other students.

1 In your country or area, do people ever wear masks? If so, why and when?

2 Do you know any films, plays or stories where masks are important?

Grammar 1: reported statements

1

1 Look at picture A. Cassia is telling her friend Pedro about her mask party. Complete what she says (in direct speech) with the correct verb from the box.

can	have	had	will

A

1 *I ... a mask party during Carnival every year.*

2 *I ... a great one last year.*

3 *I ... have a mask party for Carnival next month.*

4 *You ... come to my party.*

2 Look at picture B. Pedro is telling his friend Nico about what Cassia said. How are the reported statements (in picture B) different from the statements in direct speech (in picture A)? Complete the table below.

B

1 *She said she had a mask party during Carnival every year.*

2 *She said she had had a great one the year before.*

3 *She said she would have a mask party for Carnival the following month.*

4 *She said I could come to her party.*

	Direct speech	Reported speech
Verb tenses	present simple	
	past simple	
	will	
	can	
Time phrases	*last year*	
	next month	

2

1 The two most common verbs used for reporting statements are *say* and *tell*. Look at the two examples below. Do we need an object after *say*? Do we need an object after *tell*?

- He **said** he would take me to the airport.
- She **told** me she'd been to the doctor.

2 Complete the sentences below by writing *said* or *told*.

1 She .... she would go out on Saturday.

2 My teacher .... me that I had to do extra maths classes.

3 I .... the examiner that I didn't understand the question.

4 Polly .... she had phoned me three times.

5 You .... I could borrow your bike.

6 They .... us that they would arrive late.

▶ Grammar reference 5.1 p. 139

3 These sentences are in direct speech. Change them into reported speech.

Example: 'I saw a really good film yesterday.'
She told *me that she'd seen a really good film the day before.*

1 'I want to go on holiday next month.'
He said ....

2 'I studied Italian for three years.'
She told ....

3 'I can speak very good French.'
She told ....

4 'We'll have a party this month.'
They said ....

5 'I didn't do my English homework last week.'
She told ....

6 'I don't like Chinese food very much.'
He said ....

7 'We won't bring the car back until tomorrow.'
They said ....

8 'I can't go to the class this afternoon.'
She said ....

4

1 Write down five things that five different people have said to you in the last week. Don't write the names of the people.

Example: *He said he'd been to a really good show the weekend before.*

2 Listen to your partner's sentences. Can you guess who said each of the things?

Vocabulary 1: phrasal verbs

1

1 A phrasal verb consists of a verb plus one or more particles (such as *on*, *through* or *over*), which has a different meaning from the verb on its own. Look at these sentences. With a partner, try to work out the meaning of each of the phrasal verbs with *get*.

1 I've tried six times to *get through* to the box office.
2 Masks are used to *get round* the problem of playing different characters in the theatre.
3 Some people believe you can use magic masks to *get over* serious diseases.
4 He *got away with* being rude because his mother didn't hear.
5 I'm finding it difficult to *get by* because everything is so expensive.
6 I'm lucky because I *get on with* all my brothers and sisters.

2 Match the phrasal verbs with *get* above (1–6) with the correct definitions below (a–f).

Example: *1 f*

a) to find a way of dealing with a difficulty
b) to become healthy again after being ill
c) to have a friendly relationship with someone
d) to do something wrong and not be punished for it
e) to have enough money to buy the things you need, but not more
f) to succeed in reaching someone on the telephone

▶ Grammar reference 5.2 p. 140

2 Rewrite each of these sentences using the correct phrasal verb with *get*.

Example: I have a good relationship with everyone in my family.
I get on with everyone in my family.

1 Last time I had a cold, I recovered very quickly.
2 I don't want to be rich. I just want to be able to buy what I need.
3 When I have a problem, I usually solve it by asking my best friend for help.
4 When I reach someone's answer phone, I never leave a message.
5 When I was a child, I did really naughty things and usually escaped punishment.

3 Look again at the sentences you wrote in Exercise 2. Are they true or false for you? Tell your partner, giving details and reasons.

Reading

1 The pictures below form a well-known story, *Beauty and the Beast*. Work with another student and discuss the correct order of the pictures.

2 Tell the story with your partner. Take it in turns, referring to one picture each.

3 Now read the story. How similar is it to yours?

4

⚡ We use narrative tenses (past simple, past continuous and past perfect simple) when telling stories.

1 The verbs in italics in the sentences below are narrative tenses. Match the verbs in italics (1–3) with the names of the verb tenses (a–c).

1 As the father *was walking* back through the forest, he found a beautiful castle.
2 Then, one morning, Beauty *found* the Beast lying in the garden.
3 When she looked at the Beast, she saw that he *had turned* into the prince.

a) past simple (finished actions in the past)
b) past continuous (actions in progress in the past)
c) past perfect simple (actions which happened earlier than another past time)

2 Look again at the story of *Beauty and the Beast*. Underline two examples of each of the narrative tenses in 4.1.

5 Discuss these questions with other students.

1 What is the aim of the story? What can it help us to understand?
2 Can you think of any similar situations in real life?

Writing: story (3)

1

⚡ When you are writing a story, you need to make it interesting for the reader. To do this, you need to use a variety of sentence types and some interesting vocabulary.

Read the pairs of sentences below. How are they different? Which is more interesting (a or b)?

1 a) The father decided to go away. He wanted to earn some money.
  b) The father decided to go away because he wanted to earn some money.

2 a) The Beast was very big.
  b) The Beast was enormous and very ugly.

▶ Writing reference (Making your writing interesting) p. 150

Beauty and the Beast

1 Once upon a time, there was a man who had three daughters. The family didn't have much money and they had to work hard to survive. Only the youngest daughter tried to be brave and happy. Her name was Beauty because she was very beautiful. One day the father decided to go away and earn some money. The two eldest daughters asked for new clothes and jewellery, but Beauty said that she would just like a rose.

2 As the father was walking back through the forest, he found a large castle. In the garden, he saw some roses and remembered his promise to Beauty. As he picked one, a terrible Beast appeared, who was angry that he had taken a rose. The Beast said he would kill the man unless he could marry one of his daughters.

3 So the father took Beauty to stay at the Beast's castle. Beauty was frightened of the Beast at first, but she enjoyed her days because there were many interesting things to do. And, when she was asleep, she always had beautiful dreams about a handsome prince. In the dreams, the prince told her to distrust appearances, to let her heart guide her, and not her eyes.

4 Generally, Beauty was happy and soon she was not afraid of the Beast any more. Every evening, the Beast came to Beauty and asked if she would marry him. Every evening, Beauty said no, because although he was kind, the Beast was very ugly. Then, one morning, Beauty found the Beast lying in the garden and she thought he was dead. Suddenly, she realised that she really loved him and she began to cry. The Beast wasn't dead, however, and began to move.

5 Later that evening, the Beast came in and again asked if Beauty would marry him. This time, she said yes, and when she looked at the Beast, she saw that he had turned into the prince from her dreams and that she had rescued him. They got married the next day, and Beauty and the Prince lived happily ever after.

2 You can include a variety of sentence types by combining two short sentences with a linking word. Make one sentence from each pair of sentences below, using a word from the box.

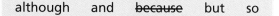

| although | and | ~~because~~ | but | so |

Example: Her name was Beauty. She was very beautiful.
*Her name was Beauty **because** she was very beautiful.*

1 He picked a rose. A terrible Beast appeared.
2 The Beast wanted to marry Beauty. Her father took her to the Beast's castle.
3 At first she was frightened. There were lots of interesting things to do.
4 The Beast was kind. He was very ugly.

▶ Writing reference (What is a sentence?) p. 147

3   Look at the words in the box. Why are they more interesting than the words in brackets in each sentence below? Complete each sentence with the correct word from the box.

~~cheerful~~   entertaining   furious
generous   enormous

Example: Only the youngest daughter tried to be brave and *cheerful* (*happy*).

1 As the father was walking back through the forest, he found an .... (*large*) castle.

2 The Beast was .... (*angry*) that he had taken a rose.

3 Beauty enjoyed her days because there were many .... (*interesting*) things to do.

4 Although the Beast was .... (*kind*), he was also very ugly.

4   You are going to write a story. Your story must begin with this sentence: *One day, I was sitting on a bench in the park when I heard someone crying.*
Decide how many paragraphs your story will have. What will the subject of each one be? Make notes for each paragraph.

► Writing reference (Planning your writing) p. 152

5   Write your story (about 100 words).

6   When you've finished writing your story, check the following things:

1 Look at all the adjectives that you have used. Could any of the words be more interesting?

2 Look at pairs of sentences. Could you combine any of the sentences to have more variety of sentence type?

3 Look at all the verbs. Have you used correct narrative tenses?

► Writing reference (Editing your writing) p. 153

Listening 2

1   Look at the photos and discuss these questions with a partner.

1 Which of the people do you think are good-looking?

2 Do you agree about all of them?

2   Listen to a radio programme about beauty and good-looking people. Tick (✓) the things the speakers talk about.

1 some good-looking famous people ☐
2 disagreement about what beauty is now ☐
3 agreement about what beauty is now ☐
4 scientific measurement of beauty ✓
5 changing opinions about beauty over time ☐
6 comparing fat and thin people ☐
7 comparing young and old people ☐

3   Listen again and for each question, choose the correct answer – A, B or C.

1   The interviewer thinks that
   A   Ben Affleck is better looking than Brad Pitt.
   B   Brad Pitt is better looking than Ben Affleck.
   C   Brad Pitt and Ben Affleck are equally good-looking.

2   The researchers went to different countries
   A   to find beautiful people.
   B   to find out if people agree about what *beautiful* is.
   C   to compare South American people with Russian people.

3   People in the different countries
   A   were shown the same photos.
   B   were shown different photos.
   C   took photos of each other.

4   Lara Jackson says that opinions about what is *beautiful* have changed
   A   in the last year.
   B   in the last three or four years.
   C   in the last 30 or 40 years.

5   Lara Jackson says that fatter people
   A   are more fashionable now.
   B   were more fashionable before.
   C   were more unhealthy before.

6   The interviewer thinks that large, fat chins are
   A   unhealthy.
   B   attractive.
   C   unattractive.

4

1   Look at these sayings (1–5) and match them with their correct meanings (a–e).

   Example: *1 e*

   1   'Beauty is in the eye of the beholder.'
   2   'You can't judge a book by its cover.'
   3   'Better a good heart than a fair face.'
   4   'Beauty is only skin deep.'
   5   'Not being beautiful is a true blessing.'

   a) Life is easier if you're not beautiful.
   b) Someone may not be a nice person just because they're beautiful.
   c) It's better to be a nice person than to be beautiful.
   d) A person's appearance doesn't tell you about their character.
   e) There are lots of different opinions about what is beautiful.

2   Work with a partner and discuss the sayings. Which ones do you agree with? Why? Do you have any similar sayings in your own language?

Grammar 2: reported questions

   1   *She asked me **who I liked** best.*

   2   *She asked me **what things beautiful people had** in common.*

   3   *She asked me **if this was** a personal opinion.*

   4   *She asked me **if I agreed** with that opinion.*

1   The woman in the picture has just finished a radio interview. The interviewer asked her a lot of questions. She is telling her friend what questions she was asked. Write the reported questions in direct speech, starting with the word given.

1   'Who *do you like best?*'
2   'What ....?'
3   'Is this ....?'
4   'Do ....?'

2   Look again at the examples in Exercise 1. How is the word order of reported questions different from the word order of questions in direct speech? Think about:

a) *Wh-* questions, and

b) *Yes/No* questions.

▶   Grammar reference 5.1 p. 139

3   There is one mistake in each reported question below. The mistakes may be in word order or verb tenses. Find the mistakes and correct them.

Example: My friend asked me where was her bag.
   My friend asked me where her bag was.

1   Jack asked his teacher when did the class finished.
2   Three people asked me how old was I.
3   The taxi driver asked me where I want to go.
4   She asked me if I did knew Michael's phone number.
5   Kate asked her mother if she seen Maria.
6   They asked me whether could I speak French.

4   Rewrite the questions below in reported speech.

Example: 'Where did you go yesterday?'
He asked me *where I had been the day before.*

1 'Do you like swimming?'
She asked me ....

2 'Who did you meet at Jim's party last week?'
My friend asked me ....

3 'Can you drive?'
He asked me ....

4 'Will you tell Gerry?'
She asked me ....

5 'What do you usually do on Friday evenings?'
They asked me ....

6 'Can you phone me this evening?'
He asked me ....

7 'Did you see your teacher yesterday?'
My friend asked me ....

8 'Where will you go on holiday next year?'
She asked me ....

Vocabulary 2: appearance

1

1 Look at the examples below. All the adjectives in italics describe physical appearance. Use a dictionary to check the meanings you're not sure of.

A
Julia Roberts is more *attractive* than Anna Kournikova.
Brad Pitt is very *good-looking*.
We all have our personal tastes about what is *beautiful*.

B
Many models think it's fashionable to be *slim*.
Some fashion models are really *thin*.
In my opinion, Kate Moss is too *skinny*.

2 Discuss the following questions.

1 In group A, which adjective is usually used for men, which for women and which can be used for both?

2 In group B, which adjective is the most polite?

2   Divide the words below into the four groups in the table. Do you know how to pronounce all of them? Check in a good English–English dictionary, if necessary.

> ~~attractive~~   ~~beard~~   beautiful   blonde
> curly   good-looking   medium height
> moustache   overweight   plain   short
> skinny   slim   straight   tall   thin
> wavy   well-built

beauty	height	weight/build	hair (face and head)
attractive			*beard*

3   Look at the pictures. Which of the words in Exercise 2 can you use to describe them?

4 Match the questions (1–8) with the appropriate answer (a–h).

Example: *1 c*

1 How *tall* is she?

2 Has he got a *beard*?

3 What's her hair like?

4 What does he look like?

5 Is she very *slim*?

6 Has he got *curly* hair?

7 Do you think he's *good-looking*?

8 Is she *beautiful*?

a) He's *short* and *well-built*.

b) Very *straight* and *blonde*.

c) *Medium height*.

d) Yes, he's very *attractive*.

e) No, it's just a bit *wavy*.

f) Yes, and a *moustache*.

g) No, she's quite *plain*.

h) More than that. I think she's *skinny* – too *thin*.

5 Work with a partner. Think of someone famous, but *don't tell* your partner who you are thinking about. Your partner should ask the questions in Exercise 3 (and any others he/she can think of) and try to guess who the person is.

Example:

　A *I'm thinking about someone famous.*

　B *What's this person's hair like?*

　A *It's long and blonde.*

　B *Is this person tall?*

Speaking

1

1 Complete the dialogue using the phrases in the box.

> Oh, I don't really agree.
> ~~I think~~
> That's right.
> I agree up to a point, but
> in my opinion,
> I don't agree at all!

A (1) *..I think....* Brad Pitt is better looking than Ben Affleck.

B (2) .... I like Ben Affleck!

A Well, (3) .... it's a matter of personal taste. Do you agree?

B (4) .... it depends on when you're talking about. Fashions change, don't they?

A (5) .... Three hundred years ago, fat chins were considered very attractive!

B Oh no! (6) ....

2 Listen to the dialogue and check your answers.

2 Look again at the phrases in the box in Exercise 1 and discuss the following questions with a partner.

1 Which two phrases do we use for *giving opinions*?

2 Which two phrases do we use for *agreeing with someone*? Which one is used for stronger agreement?

3 Which two phrases do we use for *disagreeing with someone*? Which one is used for stronger disagreement?

3

1 Read the statements below and write the number next to each one which is closest to your opinion. Think about your reasons.

1 totally agree　2 mostly agree　3 agree a bit and disagree a bit　4 mostly disagree　5 totally disagree

1 People should smile more.

2 Not enough men care about their appearance.

3 People spend too much money on make-up.

4 It's good to encourage young people to be thin.

5 Fashion magazines should include more photos of larger women.

2 Work in small groups and compare your opinions. Give your reasons.

Example:

　Student A *I think people should smile more because it makes everyone happier. Do you agree?*

　Student B *Well, I agree up to a point, but they might not feel like smiling …*

▶ Unit test 5: Teacher's Book

UNIT
6 Whatever next?

Listening 1

1 You will hear a conversation between Tom and Paola, who are talking about the Internet. Before you listen, discuss the following questions.

1 Look at the photograph. Why do you think this man is called DotComGuy? What do you think he did?

2 In what year do you think the Internet first started?

2 Listen to the conversation and answer the questions in Exercise 1.

3

1 Before you listen again, read these statements and try to decide if they are true or false. This will help you to listen for the specific information you need.

1 Paola thinks the Internet started about thirteen years ago.
2 Paola thinks that the first email was sent in 1969.
3 Tom is interested in when the first pizza was ordered on the Internet.
4 Paola prefers to do her shopping on the Internet.
5 DotComGuy spent a year without going to any shops.
6 Paola thinks watching DotComGuy on the Internet is fun.

2 Now listen again and mark each statement true or false.

4 Discuss these questions in small groups.

1 What do you think about what DotComGuy did? Would you watch him on the Internet? Why?/Why not?

2 How often do you use the Internet? What do you usually use it for?

3 What do you think about buying things on the Internet? What do you think the advantages and disadvantages are?

Example: *It's probably quick and easy, but you can't see the things properly.*

Vocabulary 1: computers

1 Look at the computer icons below and match them with the correct functions.

Example: *1 D*

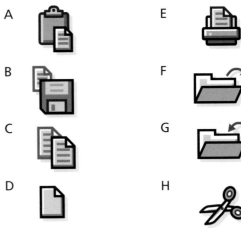

A   E

B   F

C   G

D   H

1 to open a new document
2 to open an existing document
3 to save a document
4 to close a document
5 to print a document
6 to cut
7 to copy
8 to paste

2 Complete the sentences below with the correct form of the phrases in Exercise 1.

Example: Don't *close*........ that document please – I'd like to read it first.

1 Can you .... two copies of that document before you close it, please?

2 You don't need to type that paragraph again. Just .... it and then .... it in the place you want.

3 Don't forget to .... your document before you close it.

4 Annabelle .... a new document, but she didn't give it a name.

5 'Application form' is already the name of one of your .... documents.

6 I think your essay is too long. Why don't you .... the last two paragraphs?

3 Look at the sentences below. Divide the phrases in italics into two groups.

A THINGS YOU CAN USE YOUR COMPUTER FOR

check my email

B PROBLEMS YOU CAN HAVE WITH YOUR COMPUTER

1 I *check my email* every day.

2 I *visited a* fantastic *website* last week. It showed you everything about the latest computer games.

3 I use my computer mostly for *word-processing*.

4 I didn't *make a back-up copy*. So when I *got a virus*, I lost everything.

5 I usually *send* about five *emails* a day and *receive* about seven or eight.

6 I spend quite a lot of time *surfing the Net*, but I don't usually *buy* things *online*.

7 I spent three hours writing an essay. Then my computer *crashed* and I *lost the whole document*.

4 Look again at the sentences in Exercise 3. Decide if each one is (or was) true or false for you. Compare with a partner, giving details.

Example: 1 *I usually check my email more than once a day – probably three or four times actually.*

Reading

His love is real. But he is not.

1 Look at the photos from the film *A.I. Artificial Intelligence*. If you haven't seen the film, what do you think it is about? If you have seen the film, did you enjoy it? Do you know the answers to the following questions? Discuss with a partner.

1 Who originally wrote the film?

2 When is the film set?

3 Is it a good film for young children? Why?/Why not?

2

Scanning means looking through a text quickly to find answers to specific questions. You don't need to read or understand every word to do this.

Scan the text *as quickly as you can* and find the answers to the questions in Exercise 1.

A.I.

Stanley Kubrick worked on the film *A.I. Artificial Intelligence* for nearly 20 years. After his death in 1999, he wanted Steven Spielberg to take over and direct it. The film is, therefore, an interesting mixture of terrifying Kubrick and emotional Spielberg.

A.I. is set in the distant future. Technology is very advanced and robots do many of the difficult and boring jobs humans did before. Due to the world's limited resources, however, humans have to limit the number of children they have. Monica and Henry Swinton's son becomes terminally ill. Their only way of having another child is to go to a company called Cybertronics. The company creates David, a new kind of child robot. David is programmed to love, and be loved in return by humans. These new robots can be the children that many humans could never have.

The Swintons have problems with David, however, and decide to return him to Cybertronics to have him destroyed. But at the last minute, Monica feels she can't, so she takes him to the woods and leaves him there. In the woods, David remembers the story about Pinocchio who was turned into a real boy by the Blue Fairy. David decides he's going to find the Blue Fairy who will turn him into a real boy. Then, he believes, his human family will have him back.

A.I. Artificial Intelligence includes the best of both Spielberg and Kubrick. Spielberg wants to make us feel good and tell us about things we know. But this is not a film for young children. Kubrick's frightening influence is there too. He wants to disturb us, and show us things we don't want to see.

3 Read the text again. For each question, choose the correct answer – A, B, C or D.

1 What is the writer trying to do in the text?
   A tell you not to see the film
   B describe how the film was made
   C tell the whole story of the film
   D give a general opinion about the film

2 Why would somebody read the text?
   A to decide whether to see the film
   B to find out more about robots
   C to find out about future technology
   D to learn about Kubrick's life

3 Why can't the Swintons have another human child?
   A Because their son is ill.
   B Because they are both ill.
   C Because there are restrictions on how many children you can have.
   D Because they have so many robots in the house.

4 Why does David want to be a real boy?
   A Because he wants to be like Pinocchio in the story.
   B Because he wants to go back to the Swintons.
   C Because he wants to find a fairy.
   D Because he wants to destroy Monica.

5 What is the writer's overall opinion of the film?
   A The Spielberg/Kubrick partnership didn't work well.
   B It's a good film but only for teenagers and adults.
   C It's very disturbing and he doesn't want to see it again.
   D It's a film that makes you feel good.

4 What do you think about the idea of artificial intelligence (AI)? Choose the answer – A, B or C – which is nearest to your opinion. Then compare and discuss your answers with a partner, giving reasons.

1 When do you think that artificial intelligence (e.g. like the robot, David, in the film *A.I.*) will happen? Why?
   A in 5 to 20 years' time
   B in 20 to 50 years' time
   C never

2 Do you think that artificial intelligence will be good for people? Give your reasons.
   A Yes, I think it's a great idea.
   B No, not really – it depends what it's used for.
   C No, I think it's a terrible idea.

Grammar 1: *will* and *going to*

1

1 Look at the two pictures. In which situation (1 or 2) is the decision made:

   a) at the moment of speaking?
   b) before the moment of speaking?

1

What are you going to buy Philip for his birthday?

Umm … I don't know … Well, I think I'll buy him a computer game.

2

Are you going to buy Philip a CD for his birthday?

No, I'm going to buy him a computer game.

2 Match the rules (A and B) with the correct verb forms:

   will (not) + infinitive
   am/are/is (not) going to + infinitive

> **A** Decisions made at moment of speaking:
> ....
>
> **B** Decisions made before moment of speaking:
> ....

2   Choose the correct alternatives.

1 Tim can't come. He*'ll/'s going* to see his dad.

2 I've just heard Gina's phone message. I think I*'ll/'m going to* phone her back now.

3 Your bag looks heavy. I*'ll/'m going to* carry it for you.

4 Dominic *will/is going to* bring some food. He told me this morning.

5 Oh no! It's raining. I think I*'ll/'m going to* take my umbrella.

6 I*'ll/'m going to* visit my friend in Paris. I've just got the ticket.

3   Complete these sentences. Use the correct form of *will* or *going to*.

Example: I've decided I*'m going to* be a scientist.

1 Mariko bought some paint yesterday. She .... paint her bedroom orange!

2 I suddenly feel very tired. I think I .... stay in tonight.

3 I've spoken to Angelo. He .... take me to the airport.

4 David has decided that he (*not*) .... apply for that job.

5 Oh, Ricky's here! Well, I (*not*) .... go now because I'd like to talk to him.

6 You can't walk there in this rain. I .... take you in the car.

4

1 Look at the two pictures. Both speakers are predicting a future event. In which situation (1 or 2) is the speaker using:

   a) some evidence that he/she can see now?
   b) something that he/she knows or believes?

1

Be careful with that! You're going to break it.

2

Don't lend your CD player to your brother. He'll break it.

2 Match the rules (A and B) with the correct verb forms:

   will (not) + infinitive
   am/are/is (not) going to + infinitive

> **A** Predictions about future events based on evidence you can see or hear now: ....
>
> **B** Predictions about future events based on what you know or believe: ....

▶ Grammar reference 6.1 p. 140

5 Choose the form you think is best, giving your reasons.

Example: (1) *'will' is best because you are talking about what you **believe** about that actor.*

a) That actor is always really good – I'm sure he (1) *will/is going to* be great in the new film. I'm meeting Gary at the cinema at 6.00 but I'm sure he (2) *will/is going to* arrive late. He always does.

b) It's Rita's party on Saturday. It (3) *will/is going to* be a really big party – everyone's talking about it. I'm sure she (4) *will/is going to* invite you – you're her best friend.

c) It's really freezing today and the sky is all white. I think it (5) *will/is going to* snow. The children next door (6) *will/are going to* be really pleased.

d) I haven't seen my uncle for about ten years. I wonder if he (7) *will/is going to* recognise me. I'm sure he (8) *will/is going to* look really different.

e) Be careful! You (9) *will/are going to* spill that drink. Don't get it on the carpet. My mum (10) *will/is going to* be really angry.

6   Do you agree or disagree with the predictions below? Discuss and compare with a partner.

In ten years' time …

1 I will speak English very well.

2 I will live in the same city as I do now.

3 people will use email more than now.

4 Chinese will become the most important language in the world.

5 people will study at home with computers more than now.

6 people will have holidays in space.

Speaking

1   Listen to Wojtek telling his friend Elena about his plans for the future. Which of the following questions does he talk about?

Have you got any plans for …

1 tomorrow?

2 this weekend?

3 the summer holidays?

4 next year?

5 the next five years?

2   The phrases in italics in these sentences are all ways of talking about the future. Complete each phrase using the correct word from the box. Then listen to the conversation again and check your answers.

depends	idea	like
probably	sure	thinking

1 *I'd* .... *to see* a film this weekend.

2 *We're* .... *going* to see it on Saturday.

3 *I'm not* ...., *but* I think we'll go and have a pizza on Sunday.

4 *One* .... *is to* go to France.

5 *It* .... *on* the weather really.

6 *I'm* .... *about* getting a holiday job.

3

1 Write the words in the correct order.

1 like I'd go university to to

2 thinking having party about a I'm

3 depends exam on results it my

4 probably go to travelling going I'm

5 idea is one computer a to new buy

6 sure a think I'll I'm job not get but I

2 Listen and check your answers. Repeat each sentence with the correct pronunciation.

4

1 Prepare to tell another student about your plans for the future. Think about the questions in Exercise 1. Find out any vocabulary you need.

2 Ask and answer about your future plans with a partner. Use the questions in Exercise 1 and the phrases in Exercise 2.

Vocabulary 2: collocations

1 Words that go together are called *collocations*. Some adjectives often go together, or collocate, with certain prepositions. Look at the text below. All the missing words are prepositions which collocate with the previous adjective. Choose the correct answer for each space – A, B, C or D.

Steve Grand is very good (1) .... writing computer codes. He created an amazing computer game called *Creatures*. Now, however, he isn't interested (2) .... making any more computer games. He wants to work on creating artificial intelligence. Many people are worried (3) .... how artificial intelligence will be used in the future.

1 A on   B of   C at   D with
2 A in   B of   C about D at
3 A with B in   C of   D about

2 Match the sentence parts to make complete sentences. Think carefully about the adjective/ preposition collocations.

Example: *1 j – I'm interested in learning more about the Internet.*

1 I'm interested …	a) to me.
2 She's worried …	b) from me.
3 Daniel is really good …	c) of the dark.
4 I don't know what's wrong …	d) of other people's feelings.
5 I'm keen …	e) at dancing.
6 He's not very aware …	f) to cat hair.
7 I'm very sensitive …	g) with my computer.
8 Children are often afraid …	h) about her exams.
9 Yuko is very similar …	i) on learning how to play the guitar.
10 My sister is completely different …	j) in learning more about the Internet.

3 Complete these questions with the correct preposition. Then ask and answer them with a partner.

1 What sports are you most keen ....?

2 What subjects are you good ....?

3 In your family, who are you similar ....?

4 What things (e.g. kinds of food) are you sensitive ....?

5 What kind of music are you interested ....?

6 What are you usually worried ....?

7 In your family, who are you most different ....?

8 What are you afraid ....?

Listening 2

1 The three statements about computer games below are true. Do any of them surprise you? Why?/Why not?

1 Japan is the world's biggest consumer of computer games.

2 The average age of computer games players is 28.

3 There are more computer games designers in the UK than in any other country in the world.

2 Listen to a recorded message about a computer games festival and tick (✓) the things the speaker talks about.

1 people who design computer games ☐

2 important computer games companies ☐

3 the cost of buying computer games ☐

4 the negative effects of computer games on children ☐

5 the positive effects of computer games on children ☐

6 computer games competitions ☐

7 the future of computer games ☐

3   Listen to the recorded message again. Choose the correct answer – A, B or C – for each question.

1   The festival takes place from
    A   12 to 15 June.
    B   12 to 28 June.
    C   20 to 28 June.

2   Which companies show their computer games at the New Media Centre?
    A   only British and other European companies
    B   only Japanese and American companies
    C   British, other European, Japanese and American companies

3   What percentage of children aged between 7 and 14 own a computer games machine?
    A   less than 25%
    B   about 45%
    C   more than 75%

4   Some research shows that children who are addicted to computer games are
    A   more stupid than most children.
    B   more intelligent than most children.
    C   extremely intelligent.

5   Sujoy Roy
    A   plays computer games.
    B   designs computer games.
    C   judges computer games competitions.

6   You can book by post if you pay
    A   in cash.
    B   by cheque.
    C   by credit card.

4   Discuss these questions with a partner.

1   Do you play computer games? If so, how often? Give details of what, where, when and who with.

2   Do you think it would be fun to go and watch a computer games competition? Why?/Why not?

3   Do you think computer games affect children's health and/or education positively or negatively?

4   Do you think that parents should control which computer games children play and how often they play them? Why?/ Why not?

Grammar 2: present for future

1

1   Read this dialogue. What is happening at 11.00 on Saturday morning?

A   Have you been to the computer games festival? It (1) .... on Saturday, you know.
B   I know, I really want to go.
A   Thierry and I (2) .... to the final of the competition on Saturday morning. Would you like to come with us?
B   Oh yes, great. I'd love to!
A   Well, I (3) .... Thierry there on Saturday at 10.30 and the game (4) .... at 11.00.
B   Fantastic. See you on Saturday!

2   Listen and write the correct verb in each space.

2

1   Look again at the verbs in each space in Exercise 1. What tense are verbs 1 and 4, and what tense are verbs 2 and 3?

2   Complete the rules below by writing *present simple* or *present continuous*.

> **A**   Arrangements: ....
>
> **B**   Timetables: ....

▶   Grammar reference 6.1 p. 140

3

1   Look at these sentences and decide which of them are:
    a) arrangements
    b) timetables.

    Example: I .... (*meet*) my sister at 7.30 tonight.
    Arrangement

    1   I've got the letter. My English course .... (*start*) on 15th September.

    2   I .... (*go*) swimming with Katerina on Friday afternoon.

    3   Look! It says here Tina's train .... (*arrive*) at 10.55 tomorrow morning.

4 I'm sorry I can't come; I .... (*play*) volleyball this afternoon.

5 When .... (*this programme/finish*)?

6 Maria and Dimitri told me. They .... (*have*) a party this weekend.

7 What time .... (*you/meet*) Denise tomorrow?

8 I .... (*not study*) tomorrow – I've decided to relax instead.

9 I .... (*stay*) at my grandmother's house this weekend.

10 Look at the notice. The shopping centre .... (*close*) at 8 p.m. tonight.

2 Now complete the sentences with the most appropriate form of the verb in brackets.

Example: I *'m meeting* (*meet*) my sister at 7.30 tonight. *Arrangement*

4 Work in pairs and discuss these questions. Give details in your answers, e.g. say what you're doing, when it starts/ finishes, who you're going with, etc.

Example: *I'm doing an art class on Thursday evening. I'm going with my best friend, Sara. It starts at 7.30 and it lasts for an hour and a half.*

1 Are you doing any classes this week?

2 Are you doing any sport this week?

3 Are you going out with friends this week?

4 Are you going to the cinema, the theatre, a concert or a show this week?

Writing: messages and notes

1 Discuss with other students. When do we usually write notes or messages?

Example:

People often write messages when someone phones for a person who isn't there.

I often send text messages to my friends when I want to arrange when to meet.

2 Look at these examples. Which do you think is the more appropriate style for a quick message? Why?

A
Dear Jo,
I've decided to go out with Sarah and some other friends this evening. We'll probably go to a film and then go out for a meal afterwards. I think that I will probably be back quite late.
Are you still interested in going shopping tomorrow?
I look forward to seeing you in the morning.
Love,
Tania

B
Jo,
Off to the cinema + meal with Sarah and friends tonight. Back late!
See you tomorrow a.m. for shopping!
Tania

▶ Writing reference (Formal and informal language) p. 151

3 Look at the abbreviations in italics below. What do you think they mean?

Example: Sat. = *Saturday*

1 … I'll see you *Sat. p.m.*

2 Please let me know if you're coming to the party *a.s.a.p.*!

3 My *tel. no.* is (020) 8943 5019.

4 Looking forward to seeing you on Friday. (*N.B.* We're all meeting at my place for a drink at 6.30 p.m.)

5 Bring party food, please, *e.g.* crisps, nuts, sausages, *etc.*

4 Now change these two notes so they are written in more appropriate style.

Dear Tony,
I'm writing this message to tell you that Dave phoned at about 9 o'clock this evening. He said that he was ringing to find out if you were free on Saturday because, if you are, he will get an extra ticket for the football match. He would like you to return his call at some convenient time.
Best wishes,
Paul

Dear Sally,
I am very sorry but my sister called and it is necessary for me to meet up with her this morning. Do you think you could do the shopping for the party tonight? We need all the things that we talked about. (I will pay for half of the cost of everything you buy. You will find some money in my bedroom on my desk.)
I will see you later. I hope to be home between 2 and 3 p.m. at the latest.
Love,
Eva

▶ Progress test 2: Teacher's Book

1

1 Each of these sentences has a mistake with **one** of the tenses (past simple and past continuous). Find the mistake and correct it.

1 I fell asleep while I watched the television.
2 While I travelled in Europe, I met some interesting people.
3 I saw two buses go past while I ran to the bus stop.
4 He fell off his bike while he cycled to a friend's house.

2 Each of these sentences has a mistake with **one** of the tenses (past simple and past perfect). Find the mistake and correct it.

1 Olivia offered to pay for the meal, but David already paid.
2 When I arrived, I missed the beginning of the film.
3 By the time he was four, he learned to read perfectly.
4 After closing the door, I realised I left my key in the house.

2   Complete these sentences, using the adjectives and adverbs in the box.

> beautiful   beautifully   careful
> carefully   easy   easily   happy
> happily   good   well

1 He's such a .... person – he's always laughing and smiling.
2 Please listen .... – I'm only going to say it once.
3 The test was very .... Everyone got the correct answers.
4 Francesca can speak English very .... now.
5 Look at that lovely dress! It's ....!
6 My sister likes being on her own. She sits alone .... for hours.
7 Be .... not to touch the hot cooker.
8 Are you .... at playing tennis?
9 I love her voice. She sings ....
10 I can .... run faster than you.

3   Unjumble the words to complete each description.

Tina is very (1) .... *latl* and very (2) .... *nkyins*. She's got (3) .... *dobnel*, (4) .... *vayw* hair. Most people think she is (5) .... *catervtait*.

Victor is (6) .... *dimemu getihh* and (7) .... *lewl-libut*. He's got a (8) .... *stomheuac* and a (9) .... *drabe*. He's also got (10) .... *ryclu* hair. Some people think he is (11) .... *dogo-iklogon*.

4   Complete the second sentence in each pair to report the things people said. Write one or two words in each space.

1 'I went to the cinema yesterday.'
   She told me that she had .... to the cinema the day before.
2 'I don't like listening to rock music.'
   He said he .... like listening to rock music.
3 'Do you want to play basketball with us?'
   She asked me if I .... to play basketball with them.
4 'We will try to arrive on time.'
   They said that they .... try to arrive on time.
5 'Did they see us?'
   He asked me if they .... seen us.
6 'I can fix your bike for you.'
   He said he .... fix my bike for me.
7 'Will you make the sandwiches?'
   They asked me .... I would make the sandwiches.
8 'I didn't finish my homework.'
   He told me that he .... finished his homework.
9 'Can you speak any other languages?'
   She asked me if I .... speak any other languages.
10 'I won't tell anyone.'
   He said that he .... tell anyone.

5 Choose the correct alternative – A, B or C – to complete each of these sentences.

1 I think her phone is broken. I've tried to get .... six times.
A to   B in   C through

2 She's very keen .... improving her English.
A on   B with   C to

3 It took me two weeks to get .... the flu.
A across   B over   C round

4 The film is completely different .... the book.
A to   B from   C with

5 She's very friendly and she gets .... with most people.
A over   B on   C through

6 I can't sleep. It's a problem for me and I don't know how to get .... it.
A into   B round   C out

7 My skin is very sensitive .... wool. It makes me itchy.
A on   B with   C to

8 I'm really worried .... my maths exam next week.
A about   B in   C for

9 I don't think people should get .... with dropping litter.
A over   B by   C away

10 I just had enough money to get .... on holiday.
A round   B by   C to

11 She's not always aware .... other people's feelings.
A of   B with   C for

6 Complete the dialogue with *will* or *am/is/are going to*.

Anna We must decide how everyone is going to help with the party preparations. What do you think, Sara?

Sara Yes. We've already decided that I (1) .... organise the food. And I spoke to Jenny, Mark and Kim this morning. Jenny (2) .... make all the sandwiches. Mark and Kim (3) .... buy all the paper cups and plates.

Anna Good. That's fantastic. What about the invitations?

Sara Oh, yes. Pietro's got them. He (4) .... send them today. I hope he doesn't forget. I know, I (5) .... phone him in a minute, and remind him.

Anna Yes, that's a good idea. And I think I (6) .... ask Daniel to sort out the music. What do you think?

Sara Well, I asked Charlie to do that yesterday. He (7) .... organise everything today.

Anna Fine. No problem.

Sara I (8) .... tell Daniel that he can help me with the food. There's a lot to buy and carry!

Anna OK. And I (9) .... help you with the shopping too, if you like.

Sara Thanks. I've arranged to meet Mark and Kim at the supermarket. We (10) .... meet at 3.00.

Anna OK. See you then.

7 These sentences are about timetables or arrangements. Six of them have a mistake in the tense of the underlined verb (present simple or present continuous). Find the mistakes and correct them.

1 I phoned the hairdresser and I <u>go</u> at 10.30 tomorrow morning.

2 What time <u>does</u> the film <u>start</u> on Channel 4?

3 I've arranged everything with Dina – we<u>'re leaving</u> at 6 o'clock.

4 I asked Junko to come with us, but she <u>works</u> all afternoon today.

5 Trains to Cambridge <u>are departing</u> every 30 minutes.

6 In the booklet, it says that the course <u>is finishing</u> on 21st December.

7 Maria's shop <u>doesn't close</u> until 11 p.m. on Fridays and Saturdays.

8 <u>Do</u> you <u>see</u> Caroline after the class today?

9 It says on the programme that the tour <u>starts</u> at 9 a.m. sharp.

10 I can't come to your party. I <u>stay</u> with my grandmother for the weekend.

UNIT 7

Body works

Vocabulary 1: sports

1 Put the words in the box in the correct groups below.

> crash helmet   ~~football~~
> captain   court
> basketball   pitch   umpire
> net   spectators   track
> motor racing   racket
> tennis   athletics

Sport	Equipment	People	Place
football			

2 Complete these sentences with the correct words from Exercise 1.

1 This is the third tennis .... I've broken this season.

2 The football .... is very muddy after all the rain.

3 When the ball went into the back of the ...., the crowd cheered.

4 By law, in Britain, all motor cyclists must wear a ....

5 At the end of the match, all the .... stood up and applauded.

6 He didn't agree with the decision and started arguing with the ....

7 She's an excellent .... and very good at motivating her team.

8 For the 800 m event they have to run round the .... twice.

9 They've built a tennis .... behind their house. It's great in the summer.

10 The 100 m and 200 m are my favourite .... events.

3 Four people are talking about sports they enjoy. Read what they say and name the sports.

1
> I went to hit the ball and ran straight into the net. My racket went out of my hand and across the court. I felt very stupid.

2
> I love being next to the track and watching the drivers getting ready at the start. It's great when the flag goes down and they race off.

3
> We've had a difficult season but now we've got a new manager and bought one or two new players. I hope they'll score a few goals!

4
> It's not true that you have to be tall to be good. Some of the best players at our school are quite short, but they're fast and very accurate when throwing the ball at the basket.

Watch Out *win* or *beat?*

Which of the verbs in **bold** means:

1 to be the best or first in a game or competition?

2 to defeat someone in a game or competition?

a) Do you think they will **win** the basketball tournament?

b) I **beat** my dad at tennis this morning.

4 Discuss these questions with other students.

1 Which sports do you like to watch? Which do you like to play?

2 Where do you play your favourite sport and who do you play it with?

3 Which are the three most popular sports in your country? Why do you think they are so popular?

4 Name five sports which haven't been mentioned already.

Speaking

1 Work with another student. Look at these photographs. Which of the words in the box relate to picture A? Which relate to picture B? Which could relate to both?

> to get exercise   a gym   to go jogging
> traffic   the weather   trainers
> an exercise machine   street

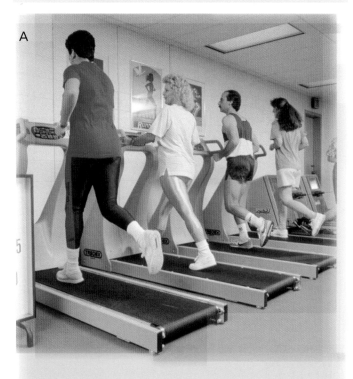

A

B

2 Listen to Carla and Gerhard talking about going to the gym and going jogging. Complete this table with their likes and dislikes.

	Carla	Gerhard
Gym	Likes ☐ Dislikes ☐ Why? Near my home	Likes ☐ Dislikes ☐ Why? ....
Jogging	Likes ☐ Dislikes ☐ Why?	Likes ☐ Dislikes ☐ Why? ....

3 Listen again and complete these sentences. They each show different ways of helping your partner to say something.

1 I can watch MTV while I do my exercise. What ....?

2 It's very peaceful in the morning. I think it's relaxing, ...?

3 So .... other kinds of exercise do ....?

4 Give your opinions about the following subjects and then ask for your partner's views, using the expressions from Exercise 3.

Example: *I like going to fast food restaurants when I'm out shopping and don't have much time. What about you?*

1 fast food restaurants

2 mobile phones

3 recycling rubbish

4 motorbikes

5 American films

5 The photographs in Exercise 1 show people exercising in different ways. Now talk with another student about the ways in which you like to get exercise and the ways you don't like. Remember to ask for your partner's views.

Reading 1

1   Work with other students.

1   Describe what you can see in each of the pictures.

2   What do you think of the Olympic Games? Are you interested in them?

3   Is training for the Olympics from an early age a good or a bad thing? Why?

2   Read the following magazine article. Which of the people think training for the Olympics from an early age:

a) is a good thing?

b) is a bad thing?

c) can be good or bad depending on different things?

Talkback – Kids and the Olympics

To become a serious Olympic competitor means taking your sport seriously from a very early age. But what does that do to a young person's life? Is it a positive or a negative thing? We sent Emma Deacon out to find the views of a number of young people.

Tara

I definitely think that going for your dreams is worth the pain and sacrifice. I'm a gymnast and I have to train 20 hours a week but I love it. I don't know what I would do without gymnastics – probably sit in front of the TV the whole time! Even if I never make it to the Olympics, I've had fun and that's what counts. I've also made some really good friends. I'm in great physical condition. I can do any sport I want to.

Rachel

If a kid really believes they can go to the Olympics or win an Olympic medal, then they should be allowed to go for it. But you should only keep doing something if it's fun. If you're not having fun, then it's not worth it. The Olympics should just be a possible bonus in the future.

Thomas

I think training for the Olympics from childhood is a really bad idea. If you're going to make it, you'll have to sacrifice your education, time, friendships and many other things. In the end, it will make you miserable. As well as that, there's always the chance of getting injured when you're training or competing.

David

Each person must decide for themselves. They mustn't be pressurised by teachers or friends and family. They should be told about what it will involve and all the training that they'll have to do. Maybe they should talk to some athletes who have made it to the Olympics to find out what they feel about it all. It's a big decision and they should think it over carefully.

3   Read the article again and decide if each of these statements is true or false.

1   Tara has no doubts that training seriously is a good thing.

2   Tara watches a lot of TV.

3   Rachel thinks young people should be advised not to aim for the Olympics.

4   Rachel thinks that having fun is important.

5   Thomas says you will lose friends because of training.

6   Thomas points out the physical risks of training for the Olympics.

7   David thinks that young people should follow the views of their families.

8   David suggests that they should talk to people who have competed in the Olympics.

4   Discuss with other students. Whose opinion in the article do you most agree with? Give reasons.

Grammar 1: *must, have to*

1   Match the examples (1–4) with the rules (A–D).

1   Our team coach is very strict. We *have to* train twenty hours a week.

2   I haven't seen my friends for ages. I *must* spend more time with them.

3   You *mustn't* be late for team practice.

4   You *don't have to* be in the team if you don't want to.

A   no obligation

B   prohibition

C   obligation from the speaker

D   obligation from outside the speaker

► Grammar reference 7.2 p. 141

2   Complete this letter with *have to*, *don't have to* or *mustn't* and a verb from the box.

do	eat	change	swim
	go	~~jog~~	

Dear Rob,

Thanks for your letter! Yes, I've made a New Year's resolution too – to get fit!

You know my brother is a sports teacher – he's worked out a training programme for me and a new diet!

First of all, I (1) ......have to jog...... for half an hour every weekday before school around the park next to my house. Then, I (2) .... 20 lengths of my local pool on Wednesday and Friday evenings and finally, I (3) .... to a yoga class on Saturday mornings.

Luckily, he's not too strict, and I (4) .... anything on Sundays, which is wonderful! I also (5) .... my diet too much but he says I (6) .... any chocolate or cakes. That's hard because you know how much I love sweet things!

I'm going to try this for the next two months and then I hope you'll see a new improved me!

Love,

Andrea

3 Rewrite each sentence using *mustn't* or *doesn't/don't have to*.

Example: Don't tell anyone. It's a secret.
*You **mustn't** tell anyone. It's a secret.*

1 It's not necessary to go up the stairs. There's a lift.
You ....

2 Hannah is not allowed to eat fish. She's allergic to it.
Hannah ....

3 There's no need for him to go to work today because it's a public holiday.
He ....

4 It's important not to be late. They close the door at 9 o'clock.
You ....

5 It's not necessary to pay to go into this museum. It's free.
You ....

4 Write down two things you *have to* do, two things you *don't have to* do and two things you *mustn't* do in your everyday life.

Example: *I **have to** get up at 6.30 a.m. on weekdays.*

Listening

1 Look at this picture and answer these questions.

1 How do you feel about tattoos? Do you like them on other people?

2 Would you ever consider having one?

2 Listen to Martin talking. Which of the following subjects does he talk about?

1 when he became interested in tattoos
2 where he lives
3 the types of tattoos people have
4 what he does in his free time
5 why he likes his job
6 the types of clients he has
7 if having a tattoo hurts
8 how much having a tattoo costs
9 if you can remove a tattoo

3 Listen again and look at the notes below about Martin. Some information is missing. For each question, fill in the missing information in the numbered space.

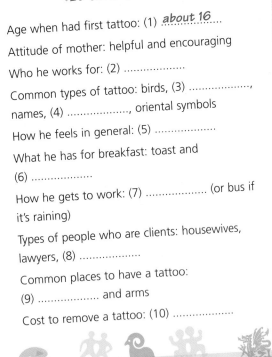

MARTIN HARRISON – TATTOOIST

Age when he had first tattoo: (1) *about 16*

Attitude of mother: helpful and encouraging

Who he works for: (2) ....

Common types of tattoo: birds, (3) ...., names, (4) ...., oriental symbols

How he feels in general: (5) ....

What he has for breakfast: toast and (6) ....

How he gets to work: (7) .... (or bus if it's raining)

Types of people who are clients: housewives, lawyers, (8) ....

Common places to have a tattoo: (9) .... and arms

Cost to remove a tattoo: (10) ....

4 Martin mentions four parts of the body. What are they?

5 Complete this puzzle with the names of parts of the body. There are clues below to help you.

						1		2
			3					
4 T	O	E		5				
		6						
7	8		9					

Across

4 one of the five parts at the end of your foot

5 the short thick finger at the side of your hand

6 the thing that covers your whole body

7 the part of your body where your foot joins your leg

Down

1 part of your body at the side of your neck where your arm joins your body

2 the lines of short hairs above your eyes

3 part of your body that joins your head to your shoulders

5 the soft part inside your mouth that moves when you eat and speak

8 the part of your face that you use for smelling things and breathing

9 the edges of your mouth where the skin is redder and darker

6 Test another student on the parts of the body by giving definitions or examples.

Example:
Student A *People often brush these in the morning and evening.*
Student B *Teeth!*

Grammar 2: requests

1 We can make requests using *can*, *could* and *would*. *Could* and *would* are usually a little more polite than *can*. Match each of the following requests (1–7) with the appropriate response below (a–g).

Example: *1 g*

1 Could you turn the music down a bit, please?

2 Can you lend me your tennis racket?

3 Would you fill out this form, please?

4 Can I have a cheeseburger, please?

5 Could I try on these jeans, please?

6 Would you open the window, please?

7 Can you clean the table, please?

a) Yes, of course. The changing room is over there.

b) Of course. It is quite hot in here.

c) Sure, but can I borrow a pen?

d) Sorry, but I'm playing Tim at 11 o'clock.

e) OK. With or without French fries?

f) No problem. I'll just get a cloth.

g) Sorry, I couldn't hear what you said.

2 Listen to the pronunciation of all the requests and their responses in Exercise 1. Practise them with a partner.

3

1 For each of these situations, make a list of the kinds of requests you can make.

Example: in a classroom: *asking another student to lend you a pen*

1 in a classroom
2 in a café
3 at home
4 on a train

2 Work with another student. Choose one request from each situation in 3.1. Take turns to make the request and give the appropriate response for each one.

Example:
Student A *Could you lend me a black pen?*
Student B *Of course. Here you are.*

Reading 2

1   These people all want to improve their health or get fit. Read the descriptions of eight books. Decide which book would be the most suitable for each person. As you read about each person, highlight or underline any important words or phrases. As you read about each book, look for parallel words or phrases that link the book to a particular person. (The first one has been done for you.)

1 Penny has been spending a lot of time working at her computer recently. She wants some ideas about how to be more active but she has very little free time.

2  Andy is feeling a lot of pressure because of exams and problems with his girlfriend. He can't relax and isn't sleeping well. It's making him depressed and he knows things must change.

3 Claire plays a lot of tennis but recently has had a problem with one of her knees. She wants to know what to do to help it heal quickly.

4  Mr and Mrs Stevens have two children aged eight and nine. It is the summer holidays and they need ideas for how to keep the children occupied.

5 Simon has been told by his doctor to try to eat more healthily but he's not sure how to change his diet.

REVIEWS Books

A   Adriana Feltz **Look Like the Stars**
An insider's guide to how some of Hollywood's most glamorous actors manage to look so good. With interviews, photographs and detailed advice, we learn what it takes to get those superstar looks.

B   Kelly Richards **Looking After No. 1**
How many of us have picked up some small injury or problem that just refuses to go away. The trouble is, if we don't do anything about it, it may just get worse. Kelly Richards has written an excellent resource book covering all sorts of minor problems that we can get and what to do about them. There is an especially good section for sports players

C   Sheila Barton **A Little Can Mean a Lot**
Under pressure from studies or work? Essays or reports to be done? Feel as if you're chained to your computer? Don't worry. Here are some tips for getting exercise in your home during short breaks. You don't have to take the whole morning off to go to the gym or swimming pool. Now you can get fit and get all your work done.

D   Dr Julian Ermord **Eat Better, Feel Better**
Here is the ideal guide from an expert to help the ordinary person take control of their eating habits and become healthier as a result. Whatever you enjoy eating at the moment, Dr Ermord will tell you what to cut down on and help you to make gentle changes to improve your diet.

E   Tania Widdowson **Mummy, I'm Bored!**
Just what you need during the long school breaks. Literally hundreds of ideas to keep the little ones busy, including lots of games for the garden which are suitable for groups of children. They're not only fun, but all that running round will wear them out and make sure they get a good night's sleep!

F   Dr Marina Tucker **The Vitamin Debate**
Have you wondered if all those different vitamin pills that you see advertised really do any good? Dr Tucker does a detailed analysis of exactly how much of each vitamin our body needs and how much we get from an average diet. Her conclusions are quite surprising!

G   Simon Montague **Body Beautiful**
If you feel fed up when you look in the mirror, here is your chance for change. In this book you will find a number of different training programmes to help you get rid of the fat and improve your muscle tone in key parts of the body. You choose where to put the effort. Believe me, it really works!

H   Dr Susie Guerin **Finding Your Inner You**
Is the stress of everyday life getting you down? Dr Guerin takes us on a journey to discover ways of bringing peace into our busy lives. Using meditation techniques from the East and with an accompanying cassette, this book is a must.

2   Which of these books would you be most interested in reading? Why? Tell another student.

Vocabulary 2: phrasal verbs

1 Look at the phrasal verbs in the dialogue and match them to the definitions below.

Example: *(1) b*

Dr So, Simon, how can I help you?

S Well, doctor, a couple of days ago I (1) **came out in** this rash ... you see these little red spots on my arm?

Dr Yes, I see. And how have you been feeling generally?

S I never have any energy. (2) **I'm worn out** all the time. And yesterday, I was picking up a box and I just (3) **passed out**. The next thing I knew, my sister was standing over me with a glass of water.

Dr You're the fourth person I've seen today who seems to (4) **have come down with** the same thing. I'm afraid there is a virus going round. If you don't mind, I'd like to (5) **carry out** a few tests.

S No, that's fine. To be honest, it's been (6) **getting me down**. I just want to know what it is. Do you think it will take long to (7) **get over**?

Dr Hopefully not, but let's wait and see what the test results are.

a) lose consciousness
b) show the signs of an illness
c) be very tired
d) recover from
e) get an illness
f) make depressed
g) do (tests, someone's instructions, etc.)

2 Complete these sentences. One word is missing in each.

1 I woke up and found I'd .... out in little bumps all over my legs.

2 My head was going round and round and I thought I was going to .... out.

3 I've been moving furniture all morning and now I'm .... out!

4 The weather's really .... me down. I hate it when it rains.

5 It's taking him longer than expected to .... over the accident.

6 We've all .... down with some kind of food poisoning. It's horrible.

7 Soldiers are trained to .... out their orders without question.

3 Discuss these questions with other students.

1 When was the last time you felt completely worn out?

2 Have you ever passed out?

3 What kinds of things get you down?

Writing: informal letter (3)

1 Look at the section on punctuation in the Writing reference on page 148. Then rewrite the following sentences with the correct punctuation.

1 she went to germany with martin on friday

2 he wrote some emails arranged a meeting spoke to his manager and then left the office

3 jeremy will eat potatoes carrots peas and tomatoes but he wont eat mushrooms

4 ill put these clothes on rachels bed

2 Read the letter. What facilities at the new leisure centre does Tim mention?

Dear Kerry,
Thank you for your letter it sounds like you had a great holiday!
I'm just writing to invite you to come with me to a great new leisure centre which has just opened near my house. It's got a huge swimming pool and courts for basketball tennis and badminton. They've also got a very modern gym and a really nice café where you can get drinks and snacks. Let me know if you're interested it would be great to see you and hear all your news!
Love,
Tim

3 Read the letter again. Correct the punctuation mistakes.

4 An interesting new place that you'd like to visit has just opened in your town. Now you are writing to an English-speaking friend to invite him or her to go there with you. Follow this plan and write your letter (about 100 words). Check that your punctuation is correct.

► Unit test 7: Teacher's Book

Dear ....,
(Thank your friend for his or her last letter.)
(Tell him or her about the new place you'd like to visit. Say what it is and what you can do there.)
(Refer to when you will next see him or her.)
Love/Best wishes,
....

Reading

1 Look at the photos and the dictionary extract and discuss these questions.

1 In A, who is the actor? What is the film?

2 In the film, he spent four years trying to survive on a desert island. What things do you think he found difficult?

3 In B, where do you think these people are and why?

4 What do you think the connection is between the two photos?

2 Read the article about the people in picture B and answer the questions.

1 Where are they? Why?

2 How are they different from the person in picture A?

3

1 The text is divided into three paragraphs. Each has a topic sentence (usually at or near the beginning of the paragraph). Find the topic sentence for each paragraph.

A topic sentence tells you what each paragraph is about. This makes it easier to understand the whole text.

► Writing reference (Paragraphs) p.149

castaway /ˈkɑːstəweɪ/ *n* someone who is alone on an island after their ship has sunk

Castaway 2000

1 In the year 2000, a television company did an experiment called Castaway 2000. The idea was to learn about how people live together. Thirty-six people became 'castaways' on a Scottish island for a year. They had no television, radio, computers, transport or shops and only two small
5 buildings. For the whole year, they lived as a closed community. They grew and made everything they needed. They weren't real castaways, however, because a television camera filmed them. The details of their lives were on television every week.

2 One of the 'castaways' was Roger Stephenson. He was there with his
10 wife, Rosemary, and their two young sons. They taught the seven children on the island themselves. Roger says, 'I've never lived like this before. It was fantastic. The freedom really helped our children to develop. We've already decided that we want to continue to teach them ourselves. I'd like to live like this again. But I wouldn't like to be controlled by a television company
15 again.' Rosemary adds, 'I've just seen some of the programmes of us, and I didn't like **them**. The editing of the programmes made us look like very difficult people – it was very unfair.'

3 Two other castaways were a couple, Dez and Liz. Both of them are hard-
20 working people and they learned a lot about themselves. Liz says, 'The practical things were easy for me. But living with 30 other people was hard work.' In the end, however, they were both positive. 'We haven't decided where yet, but we'd like to continue to live a self-sufficient way of life,' says Dez.

2 Read these questions. Which paragraph does each refer to?

Example: *Question 1 – Paragraph 1*

1 Why did the television company create the *Castaway 2000* programme?
   A to create a 'fantasy' holiday
   B to find out more about society and communities
   C to employ people to build accommodation on the island
   D to look after the animals on the island

2 Why was there a television camera on the island?
   A to teach the people how to use television cameras
   B to give the people something to do
   C to make films about the animals living there
   D to make films about the people living there

3 What was Roger's opinion of the year on the island?
   A He liked everything about it.
   B It was good for his children, but not for him.
   C He liked the life, but he didn't like the television company being in charge.
   D He liked it at first, but not at the end.

4 What does *them* in line 16 refer to?
   A the other adults on the island
   B the other children on the island
   C the people in the television company
   D the television programmes of *Castaway 2000*

5 What was Rosemary's opinion of the television producers?
   A they were very difficult people
   B they gave the wrong impression about her family
   C they were very good at their job
   D they were very kind

6 What was the most difficult thing for Liz?
   A being in a community with lots of other people
   B leaving the island at the end of the year
   C the physical work on the island
   D learning about herself

3 Read the article again and choose the correct alternative for each of the questions in 3.2.

Grammar 1: present perfect

1   Look at the picture and the underlined verbs. Match the verbs with the correct rules (A and B).

Where's the most interesting place you've lived, Grandad?

Well, I've lived in some strange places in my life. When I was 25, I lived for a year on an island with a small group of people. We grew all our own food. The whole experience changed my life and I still grow my own vegetables!

A

Past simple: an action at a definite time in the past

B

Present perfect: an action or experience at an indefinite (or unknown) time in the past

▶ Grammar reference 8.1 p. 141

2   Look at these sentences, which use the present perfect. Six have mistakes with word order. Find the mistakes and correct them. Use Grammar reference 8.2 *ever, never, already, yet, just* on page 142 to help you.

Example: She's eaten never spaghetti. ✗
*She's **never eaten** spaghetti. ✓*

1 Have you lived ever in an unusual home?
2 We haven't finished moving the furniture yet.
3 Has she yet done the shopping?
4 Already I've bought some more bread – look, it's there!
5 He just has decided to move house.
6 Have ever you grown your own vegetables?
7 I've never been to the USA.
8 She's finished already making the dinner.

3   Complete the dialogue with the correct form of the present perfect or past simple, using the words in brackets.

A Have (1) *you ever been* (you ever be) to Australia?
B No, I (2) .... (never be) outside Europe.
   (3) .... (you be) there?

65

A   Well, no, not yet. But my parents
(4) .... (*just book*) a holiday to
Australia for next month. I'm so excited! They
(5) .... (*tell*) me about it last week.
I still can't believe it's true.

B   Wow! You're really lucky! (6) ....
(*you do*) your packing yet?

A   No, I (7) .... (*not do*) any packing
but I (8) .... (*already write*) a list of
things to buy. Yesterday I (9) ....
(*buy*) some film for my camera.

4   Write the words in the correct order to
make questions. Then ask and answer the
questions with a partner.

1   ever exciting done the thing you've What's
most ?

2   you never to do done that What have
you'd like ?

3   any Did New Year resolutions make you ?

4   yet New broken Year resolutions Have your any
you of ?

Vocabulary 1: town/country

1   Work with a partner and discuss these
questions.

1   Name the two most important cities in your
country. What is each one famous for?

2   What is the countryside like near where
you live?

2   Match the words in the box with the
correct definitions.

> built-up   crowded   facilities
> nightlife   open space   ~~peaceful~~
> polluted   public transport   traffic

Example: 1 *peaceful*

1   *adj* calm and quiet
2   *adj* full of people
3   *adj* with lots of buildings
4   *adj* dirty and dangerous (air, water or land)
5   *n* services that are available in a place
6   *n* buses, trains, etc. that everyone can use
7   *n* areas with no buildings (e.g. fields and parks)

8   *n* the number of cars, buses, etc. that are on the roads
9   *n* all the entertainment that is available in the evenings in a big town

3

1   Katia's family are preparing to move house. She is
talking to her friend, Pietro, about it. Listen and
answer the questions.

1   Is Katia moving from the country to a city or from a
city to the country?

2   Is she happy about moving?

2   Work with a partner. Try to complete the extracts
below with the words from Exercise 2. Then listen
again and check your answers.

1   There aren't many people – it isn't too (1) *crowded* .
It's very (2) .... actually, and I really like living in a
place that has plenty of (3) .... You know, it
isn't too (4) .... It's great being able to breathe
really fresh air too! There isn't much (5) .... and
it's really not (6) .... at all.

2   It's really boring! There aren't many (7) ....
I mean, you have to travel a long way to go to things
like the swimming pool, or shopping centres, you
know. And the (8) .... isn't very frequent
either, so you have to use a car a lot.

3   The place we're moving to has really good
(9) ...., so I'm really looking forward to going
out to the cinema and clubs.

4

1   Look again at the extracts in Exercise 3.2. Use the
ideas to complete the table below.

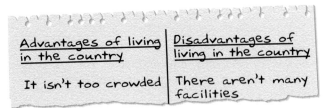

Advantages of living in the country	Disadvantages of living in the country
It isn't too crowded	There aren't many facilities

2   Now compare your lists with a partner. Can you add
any other ideas to each list?

5   Work in small groups and discuss these questions.

1   What do you like about where you live? Is there anything
you don't like?

2   If you live in the country, how often do you go to a town?
Why?
If you live in a town, how often do you go to the
country? Why?

Speaking

A

B

C

D

1

⚡ When you are describing a photograph, you can describe details of what is in the photograph and where it is.

The phrases in italics in the sentences below describe where things are in pictures A and B. What phrases express the opposite meaning for each one?

Example: on the right – *on the left*

Photo A

1 It looks strange because I can see that the blinds *on the right* are *at the bottom* of the windows.

2 The front of the building doesn't look *the right way up*.

Photo B

3 There are trees *in the background* of the picture. Perhaps it's a wood or a park.

4 The tall stilts *under* the building may be because of the weather.

5 It's possible that the woman in the picture made the piece of modern sculpture *in front of* one of the stilts.

2   Look at pictures C and D below and discuss these questions with a partner.

1 Which of the homes in the box below describe which photograph?

> bedsit   block of flats   bungalow
> cottage   detached house
> terraced house

2 Which of the homes in the box can you find in your country?

3   Write two sentences about picture C and two sentences about picture D using the phrases in Exercise 1.

4   Talk to a partner about one of the photographs – A, B, C or D. Don't forget to organise your comments.

1 First, summarise the content of the photograph.

2 Then, say where you think the photograph was taken and why.

3 Then, talk about some details. Describe what you can see in the photograph and where it is. Use the phrases and sentences in Exercise 1 to help you.

Writing: transactional letter (1)

1 Look at the task below and answer these questions.

1 Who will you write to?

2 Will you include information given to you in the task?

3 Will you include your own opinion?

4 How many words will you write?

Task

You are studying in Britain at the moment. A friend from your country is coming to study in Britain next month too. He/She would like to know about two different cities so that he/she can choose which one to go to. Write a letter to your friend. In your letter, you should:

- give some information about Edinburgh
- give some information about Brighton
- suggest which city you think is the best and why.

Write a letter using 100–120 words in an appropriate style.

Edinburgh

very friendly people

Scottish accent difficult to understand

interesting places to visit

expensive public transport

Brighton

cheaper public transport

beaches - free

not as many tourist places

good funfair

nice cafés

2 Look at the sample answer below. A student has written part of the letter and the student's teacher has indicated four problems. What four things are missing from the letter?

Nina, ← starting a letter?

Thank you for your letter. ...and?

In Edinburgh, the people are very friendly but I think the Scottish accent is difficult to understand. Although there are lots of interesting places to visit, the public transport is very expensive. In Brighton, on the other hand, the buses are quite cheap and the beaches are free! There aren't as many tourist places in Brighton. There is, however, a good funfair and lots of nice cafés.

Sonia ← last paragraph?
finishing a letter?

3

1 Look at the two sentences below. Are they expressing similar views or contrasting views?

The people are friendly.
The Scottish accent is difficult to understand.

2 Look back at the letter in Exercise 2. What is the 'linker of contrast' used to combine the two sentences above?

3 Find three more linkers of contrast in the letter.

▶ Writing reference (Making your writing interesting) p. 150

4 Look at the pairs of sentences (a and b) below. Decide if both sentences are correct or if only one is. Think about the word order and punctuation.

1 a) Although she was feeling ill, she went to work.
b) She went to work although she was feeling ill.

2 a) He studied hard but he didn't pass the exam.
b) He studied hard, but, he didn't pass the exam.

3 a) It rained on my holiday. However, I enjoyed myself.
b) It rained on my holiday, however, I enjoyed myself.

4 a) Skiing is fun. On the other hand, it's expensive.
b) Skiing is fun, on the other hand, it's expensive.

5   Rewrite these sentences, using the linkers of contrast in brackets.

1 I leave the house on time. I'm often late for school. (*although*)

2 We went to Paris. We didn't see the Eiffel Tower. (*but*)

3 I like learning English. I sometimes find it difficult. (*however*)

4 There aren't any cinemas. There are lots of sports facilities. (*on the other hand*)

6   Read the task below and write your letter. Look back at the letter in Exercise 2 and the linkers of contrast in Exercises 3 and 4 to help you.

Task

You are studying in Britain. A friend from your country is coming to visit you. She would like to know about two different areas so that she can choose which one to visit. Write a letter to your friend:

- giving some information about the Lake District and the Norfolk Broads
- suggesting which area you think is the best and why.

Write a letter using 100–120 words in an appropriate style.

Lake District
lots of mountains for walking
very beautiful
you need a car
often raining

Norfolk Broads
no mountains (very flat)
lakes and rivers for boating
some public transport
quite expensive

7   Work with a partner. Read your partner's letter and check that he/she has:

1 started and finished the letter correctly

2 included all the information asked for

3 included his/her opinion or suggestions

4 written the correct number of words.

Listening

1   Look at the cartoon and discuss these questions about your daily routines, explaining your reasons.

1 Do you usually do things in the same order? Talk about these things and say why/why not.
- getting up in the morning
- starting work (or study)

2 Do you have the same thing for breakfast and lunch every day? Why?/Why not?

3 Do you go on holiday to the same place every year? Why?/Why not?

2   Listen to two friends, Anna and Oliver, discussing routines. Do they have the same opinion or different opinions?

3

It will help you to understand conversations better if you can decide what is a fact (information that is true) and what is an opinion (what someone thinks).

Look at the following extracts from Anna and Oliver's conversation. Decide if they are opinions or facts.

Example: 'It's really interesting.' *opinion*

1 'That's amazing!'

2 'I think that's really boring.'

3 'Some people like things to be the same.'

4 'Diana always has a sandwich.'

5 'It's awful.'

6 'They obviously enjoy it.'

4

1 Before you listen again, decide what kind of information or type of word (e.g. number, place, age, adjective, noun, etc.) is missing in each of the spaces.

Example: 1 *number*

1 The man in the article has stayed in the same hotel for the last .... years.

2 Oliver likes going to .... on holiday.

3 Anna says that some people like their daily .... to be the same.

4 George and Diana have had .... in the same café for 30 years.

5 Diana always has a .... in the café.

6 George always has .... in the café.

7 George and Diana started eating in the café aged about ....

8 Oliver thinks that having the same routine is really ....

2 Now listen again and complete the sentences in 4.1.

Example: 1 The man in the article has stayed in the same hotel for the last *nine* years.

5   Read these two opinions about routines. Work with a partner and discuss which one you agree with and why.

'I think it's really depressing. They haven't had many different experiences in life.'

'I think it's OK. They obviously enjoy it and they know what they're going to get.'

Grammar 2: present perfect (unfinished past)

1   Look at the example sentences and diagrams (1 and 2) below. They show another use of the present perfect. Match them with the correct rules (A and B).

1 *Bob and Jane have had breakfast in that café for 30 years.*

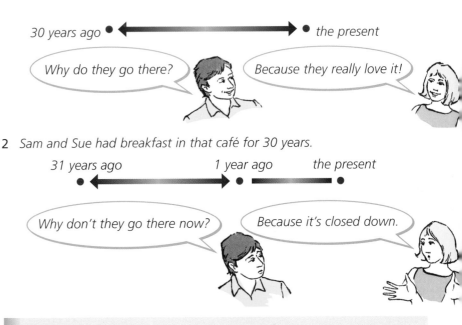

2 *Sam and Sue had breakfast in that café for 30 years.*

A Past simple: actions or situations that began and finished in the past.

B Present perfect: actions or situations that continue from the past until now.

2

1 Look at the pairs of examples below. Work with a partner and say why one is correct and one is incorrect.

1 They've had breakfast in the same café for 30 years. ✓
2 They have breakfast in the same café for 30 years. ✗
3 He's been to the same hotel for nine years. ✓
4 He's been to the same hotel since nine years. ✗
5 How long have you lived here? ✓
6 How long time have you lived here? ✗

2 Look at the examples below and complete the rules (A and B) by writing *for* and *since*.

1 He's lived in that house for five years.
2 He's lived in that house since 2001.

A We use .... when we are talking about how long something has lasted.

B We use .... when we are talking about when something started.

3 Choose the correct word: *for* or *since*.

Example: They've lived here *for*/*since* two years.

1 I haven't seen Jim *for*/*since* a week.
2 I've had a headache *for*/*since* I woke up.
3 Amy's been in hospital *for*/*since* May.
4 I've had English lessons *for*/*since* June.
5 He's had his new computer *for*/*since* months.
6 I haven't seen him *for*/*since* 10 o'clock.

4 Complete these sentences with the correct form of the verb: present perfect or past simple.

Example: I live in New York now. I*'ve lived* (*live*) here for six years.

1 Billie is a good friend of mine. I .... (*know*) her since I was nine.
2 My aunt works in a shop. She .... (*work*) there for two years.
3 That's a lovely jacket! How long .... (*you have*) it?
4 They live in Madrid now. They .... (*live*) in Rome for ten years.
5 He doesn't play football now. He .... (*not play*) football since he broke his leg.
6 How long .... (*you be*) in this class?

5

1 Complete these sentences about you.
   1 I live … (e.g. in Rome, in a flat)
   2 I've got … (e.g. a bike, a dog)
   3 I usually go … (e.g. to work by bus)
   4 My best friend is … (e.g. Denise, in America)

2 Now work with a partner. Listen to your partner's sentences and ask questions with *How long …?*
   Example:
   A *I live in Rome.*
   B *How long have you lived in Rome?*
   A *I've lived there for about four years. Before that I lived in a small town.*

Vocabulary 2: -ed/-ing adjectives

1 Look at the adjectives in italics in the table below. Which group of adjectives describe:

1 things, experiences, events?   2 people's feelings?

Adjectives ending -*ed*	Adjectives ending -*ing*
Examples: I'm really *interested* in this article. They must be so *bored*!	Examples: This article is really *interesting*. The whole weekend was really *boring*.

2 Complete each sentence with the correct adjective.

1 *confused/confusing*
   a) These instructions are very .... I can't understand them at all.
   b) He needs help with his maths homework; he's very ....
2 *surprised/surprising*
   a) It was .... to see Sonia at the party. I didn't think she would come.
   b) The book cost a lot. I was .... it was so expensive.
3 *bored/boring*
   a) The lesson was really .... because we didn't have anything to do.
   b) Sam was .... by the film. There was no action.
4 *frightened/frightening*
   a) When I was a child, I was .... of the dark.
   b) My most .... experience is going to the dentist.
5 *annoyed/annoying*
   a) She was .... because her boyfriend didn't phone her all weekend.
   b) It's so .... when people whistle all the time.
6 *excited/exciting*
   a) Your trip to Australia sounds really .... You're so lucky!
   b) Ben is really .... His girlfriend is coming home tomorrow.

3 Choose two pairs of adjectives from Exercise 2. Think of an experience for each pair. Tell your partner about the experiences and how you felt.

Example: *annoyed/annoying*

   My mum has a really annoying habit. She sings in the car. I get really annoyed and tell her to stop!

▶ Unit test 8: Teacher's Book

More than words

1 Look at the pictures and discuss this question with other students: What different ways can you communicate with other people?

2 Read this article quickly. In which parts of the world does it say that whistling is used for communicating?

Language of the birds

Eusebio Martinez was standing in (1) *front* of his hut one day. He was whistling to a man who was going to market to sell corn leaves. The man was a (2) .... way away. The man (3) .... Eusebio's whistle with a whistle. They repeated this exchange (4) .... times with different whistles. Finally, the man turned and came to Eusebio's hut. (5) .... saying a word, he showed Eusebio the corn leaves. Eusebio looked at them, went into his hut, returned with some money and (6) .... the man for the corn leaves. They had not spoken a word.

This conversation took (7) .... between Mazateco speakers. The Mazateco Indians come from Oaxaca in Mexico and use whistling to exchange greetings or buy and sell goods. Mazateco children learn to whistle (8) .... as soon as they can talk. Some of the Mazateco can actually whistle in two languages – their own Indian dialect and Spanish.

There are also other regions of the world where people 'talk' by whistling, for example, parts of north eastern Turkey and La Gomera, one of the Canary Islands. There are (9) .... people in these mountainous areas and they would (10) .... to walk for two hours to speak to their neighbours. (11) ...., they simply whistle.

3 Read the article again and choose the correct word for each space. (Before you look at the alternatives below, write down what you think the missing word is in each case.)

	A	B	C	D
1	next	behind	opposite	*front*
2	high	distant	far	long
3	answered	replied	responded	said
4	lots	several	number	much
5	Unless	Besides	However	Without
6	spent	bought	gave	paid
7	situation	position	place	time
8	near	quite	almost	until
9	little	few	alone	rare
10	necessary	must	obliged	have
11	Instead	Although	Nevertheless	Moreover

...Dear Sir, ... Waterhouse

Grammar 1: relative clauses (1)

1

1 Look at these example sentences. Each of the b) sentences contains a defining relative clause in the second half of the sentence. (We use defining relative clauses to say exactly which person or thing we are talking about.)

1 a) He was whistling to a man. The man was going to market.
   b) He was whistling to a man <u>who was going to market</u>.

2 a) Did you get the message? I sent it to you yesterday.
   b) Did you get the message <u>which I sent you yesterday</u>?

3 a) Oaxaca is a place in Mexico. The Mazateco Indians come from there.
   b) Oaxaca is a place in Mexico <u>where the Mazateco Indians come from</u>.

2 Now answer these questions.

1 In 1b) which words are replaced by *who*?
2 In 2b) which word is replaced by *which*?
3 In 3b) which word is replaced by *where*?
4 Are commas used in the b) sentences?

2 Join these sentences using *who*, *whose*, *which* or *where*.

1 The book is about a young man. The young man travels around the world.
2 Have you got the pen? I lent it to you yesterday.
3 That's the café. We went for a drink there last night.
4 He was the man. I bought his corn leaves.
5 I don't like the new boy. He is tall and has long black hair.
6 She works for a company. It makes microchips for computers.
7 Here is a photo of the party. I met my new boyfriend there.
8 They are the people. Their flight was cancelled.

Watch Out *that* (1)

Are one or both alternatives possible in each of these sentences?

1 The family *who/that* live opposite are very nice.
2 The lift *which/that* broke down is working now.

3 When *who*, *which*, etc. is the **object** of the verb, you can leave it out of the sentence. When *who*, *which*, etc. is the **subject** of the verb, you can't leave it out. Put brackets ( ) around the words in italics if they are not necessary.

Example:

$\overset{S}{}$ $\overset{O}{}$
The boy who gave me this book is my best friend. (*who* is the subject of the verb *gave*, so it is necessary)

$\overset{O}{}$ $\overset{S}{}$
The shoes (which) I bought yesterday aren't very comfortable. (*which* is the object of the verb *bought*, so it is not necessary)

1 Where is the newspaper *which* was in the living room?
2 These are the keys *that* I was looking for.
3 The girl *who* lives next door has a motorbike.
4 The village *where* I was born has a beautiful old church.
5 What was the name of the CD *which* you bought yesterday?
6 Losing my job is the best thing *that* has ever happened to me.
7 The guy *who* I met on holiday sent me an email last night.
8 Do you know a shop *where* I can get an English newspaper?

4 Complete these sentences as appropriate. Then tell another student.

Example: 1 My best friend is someone who *knows how to make the best chocolate cake in the world!*

1 My best friend is someone who ....
2 My home town is somewhere that ....
3 Reading novels is something which ....
4 Going out with my friends is something which ....
5 Watching football on TV is something which ....

► Grammar reference 9.1 p. 142

Vocabulary 1: sounds

1   Listen to the sounds on the recording and match each one to one of the verbs below.

whistle

sneeze

yawn

whisper

crash

scream

ring

bang

2   Decide if each of the words in Exercise 1 can be made by: a) a person, b) an animal or c) a thing.

3   Complete each of these sentences with one of the words from Exercise 1 in the correct form.

Example: I've got a terrible cold and I can't stop *sneezing.*

1   There was a loud explosion and then the noise of people ....

2   I'm sorry to keep .... but I didn't get much sleep last night.

3   It's no good .... I can hear every word you're saying.

4   Someone keeps .... our front door bell. I think it's the children from across the road.

5   The tray with all the glasses fell to the floor with a loud ....

6   Simon always .... to himself when he's feeling nervous.

7   The fireworks went off with a .... and everyone jumped.

4   Listen very carefully. What different sounds can you hear around you?

Listening 1: song

1   You will hear a song by Ronan Keating. One of the lines is: *You say it best when you say nothing at all.* What do you think this means?

2   Check that you know the meanings of the words in the box below. Then decide where in the song you think they should go.

> said   speak   talking   hear
> says   know   explain   saying (x2)
> define

3   Listen to the song and check your ideas.

4   Listen to the song again and follow the words. Then answer these questions.

1   How does the singer feel?
2   Do you like the song?

When you say nothing at all

It's amazing how you can (1) ....
   right to my heart
Without (2) .... a word,
   you can light up the dark
Try as I may, I can never (3) ....
What I (4) .... when you don't
say a thing

Chorus
The smile on your face lets me
(5) .... that you need me
There's a truth in your eyes (6) ....
   you'll never leave me
The touch of your hand (7) .... you'll
   catch me whenever I fall
You say it best, when you say nothing at all

All day long I can hear people (8) .... out loud
But when you hold me near, you drown out the crowd
Try as they may, they can never (9) ....
What's been (10) .... between your heart and mine

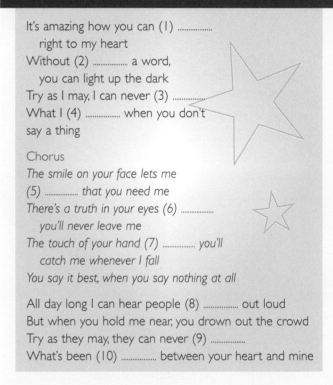

74

Reading

1   Read these descriptions of the experiences of four students who have tried different methods of learning English. Which of the people are:

1 very positive about their experience?

2 quite positive about their experience?

2   Read the text again and answer these questions.

Which person

● needed better English for work? (1) *Rajmund*....

● learned other skills in English? (2) ....

● didn't always find the method very interesting? (3) ....

● likes the flexibility of the method? (4) ....

● finds the situation quite hard work? (5) ....

● had to repeat out loud after a cassette? (6) ....

● liked the social aspect of the method? (7) ....

● studies in the afternoons? (8) ....

● thought the method was quite expensive? (9) ....

3   Which of the methods of learning English would you be most interested in? Why? Discuss this with other students.

Pierre

I wasn't doing very well in my tests at school, so my parents sent off for a set of cassettes to help me improve. They had seen an advertisement in the newspaper which promised to make you fluent in a month! You repeat after the cassette and read from a book at the same time. The book has different texts in English on one side with a translation on the other so you always understand what you are reading. I quite enjoyed reading aloud at first, but then it got a bit boring. The other thing you were supposed to do was to play the cassette just as you were going to sleep at night. That was good as it didn't need any effort at all! I suppose I did learn some things, especially some new phrases, and I do think my pronunciation improved but I'm not sure it was worth all the money my parents paid for it.

Lia

Last summer I went on this fantastic 'English activity holiday' in Scotland. Basically, I went and stayed with a Scottish family for two weeks. I had to choose between several different types of activities. In the end I picked horse-riding and photography. Every day we spent the mornings doing horse-riding and the afternoons doing photography, but all in English! I got my own horse for the two weeks and we got practice in different kinds of riding skills. I loved it! In the afternoons we were taught some theory about how to take good photos and how to develop films in a darkroom. Then we went to some beautiful places and actually took some photos. In the evenings there was always a different kind of social event like Scottish dancing. I had a great time, made lots of friends and feel a lot more confident with my English now.

Rajmund

I work for a bank and recently have had to do a lot of travelling to English-speaking countries for my job. The bank decided they wanted me to improve my English, but it's difficult for me to go to classes because I am so busy at work. So, I've been having classes over the Internet. It's an excellent system. I can log on to the RealEnglish.com website whenever I want and practise my grammar, read articles and so on. Then, when I'm ready, I can connect to a real teacher and have a lesson. I have a camera connect to a real teacher and have a lesson. I have a camera attached to my computer so I can see the teacher and she can see me. The teachers are available 24 hours a day, so I can choose to have a lesson when it suits me. It's really convenient and my English has definitely got better. I think lots of people will be learning like this soon.

Sylvia

I've been living in England for nearly six months now. I'm working as an au pair with a family in Oxford. The couple are quite nice and have a four year old who I look after during the day when her parents are at work. The mother comes home at 2 p.m. and then I go to my language class at a nearby school. It's working out pretty well. Living with an English family means I have to speak English all the time and the language classes give me a chance to work on my grammar and improve my vocabulary. It's quite tiring though, especially when I have homework to do. I am thinking about taking the First Certificate exam next year but I'm not sure.

Speaking: negotiating

1   Imagine a friend of yours is moving to another country for at least a year. What going away present might you buy them?

2   Listen to a group of young people trying to decide what to buy a friend who is going to move to Italy. What do they finally decide to buy her?

3   Listen again and complete these sentences with the negotiating phrases in the box.

> bad idea   interesting suggestion
> really good idea   how about
> why don't we   what about

1   Well, ... some kind of Italian language learning course?

2   Yes, that's an .... , but do you know how expensive they are?

3   In that case, ... a new CD Walkman?

4   Yeah, that's not a ...., but I'd like to get her something to do with Italy.

5   I know. .... get her some nice travel books about Italy?

6   Excellent! That's a ....

4   Have a conversation beginning with the questions below. Use phrases from Exercise 3 as appropriate.

Example:
Student A *What are we going to do after school today?*
Student B *Why don't we go swimming?*
Student A *That's a really good idea!*

1   What are we going to do after school today?

2   Where are we going to have lunch?

3   What film are we going to see?

4   What are we going to get Monica for her birthday?

5   Work with another student. You and your partner have won a competition which allows you both to go and study English in the English-speaking country of your choice for one month. Talk together about which country you would like to go to and why. Look at the pictures below for ideas.

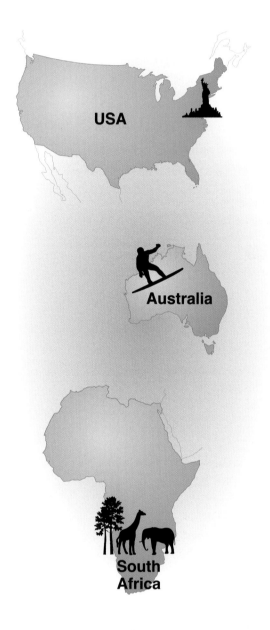

USA

Australia

South Africa

6   Tell other students what you decided and why.

Listening 2

1   Discuss these questions.

1 What different languages can you speak? How have you learned them?

2 How do you think parents with different first languages should bring up their children? Should they:
- just use one language at home?
- each speak their own language to the children?
- insist the children speak both languages at home?

2   You will hear a conversation between a girl, Natalia, and a boy, Julian. Listen and decide how well Natalia and her two sisters (Isabella and Christina) each speak Spanish.

3   Now, listen again and choose the correct option in each case.

1 Natalia's parents met
   A in London.
   B in Alicante.
   C in Barcelona.

2 How often did Isabella's dad speak to her in Spanish?
   A all the time
   B occasionally
   C never

3 Isabella went on holiday to Spain
   A every year.
   B twice a year.
   C every other year.

4 How often did Christina's mum speak Spanish to her?
   A all the time
   B some of the time
   C never

5 How often did Natalia go to Spain in her summer holidays?
   A every summer
   B quite often
   C not very often

6 Natalia would like to improve her Spanish before she goes
   A to college.
   B on holiday.
   C to Barcelona.

Grammar 2: relative clauses (2)

1

1 Look at these example sentences. The clauses in bold give us extra information about the main part of the sentence. (Notice that commas usually come before, and sometimes after, these clauses.)

   1 He met my mum, **who was brought up in Alicante,** in a club.
   2 In my school holidays I was doing a lot of horse-riding, **which I really loved.**

2 Complete each of the clauses below with *who*, *which*, *when*, *where* or *whose* as appropriate.

1 My Uncle David, ...works for IBM, lives in Manchester.

2 York, ...my best friend lives, has a marvellous cathedral.

3 My parents' house, ...they bought last year, looks fantastic.

4 I bought them at the supermarket, ...I saw Suzanne.

5 Tom told me about his new job, ...he's enjoying very much.

6 Sam, ... car had broken down, was in a very bad mood.

► Grammar reference 9.1 p. 142

2   For each question, combine the two sentences to make one sentence, using a relative clause. The sentence in brackets is the one that gives extra information. Use this to make the relative clause.

Example: Anna is studying economics. (She lives in the flat upstairs.)
Anna, who lives in the flat upstairs, is studying economics.

1 Dublin has always attracted a lot of tourists. (I was born there.)

2 Terry finally arrived at 8 p.m. (He was already half an hour late.)

3 My next-door neighbour is leaving. (I've always been afraid of his dog.)

4 We stayed in this fantastic hotel in Istanbul. (A friend had recommended it to us.)

5 Professor Burton is going to be my tutor next term. (I've always respected him.)

6 I'm going to visit friends in Mexico City. (I used to live there.)

7 My friend Simon has said I can stay in his flat. (His job means he is away a lot.)

8 A new car park will be built here by the end of the year. (It will have space for 5,000 cars.)

> **Watch Out**   *that* (2)
>
> Are one or both alternatives possible in each sentence below?
>
> 1 Michael, *who/that* I saw yesterday, is getting married at the weekend.
> 2 Her new school, *which/that* she loves, has a very good basketball team.

3   Work with another student. Write down the names of five well-known people, places and things. Say one of your words and add a non-defining relative clause. Your partner then finishes the sentence. Take it in turns.

Example:
  Student A *Chocolate, which I'm addicted to, …*
  Student B *is great for making you feel good.*
  Student B *Tom Cruise, who starred in 'Eyes Wide Shut', …*
  Student A *used to be married to Nicole Kidman.*

Vocabulary 2: phrasal verbs

1   Each of these sentences contains a phrasal verb in italics. At the end of each one there are two possible meanings of the phrasal verb. Decide on the correct meaning in each case and underline it.

Example: He had problems *getting* his message *across* to the audience. (to listen/<u>to communicate</u>)

1 I've been trying to *get through* to my bank manager on the phone all day. (to make contact with/to avoid)

2 Could you *speak up*, please? I can't hear very well. (to speak more quietly/to speak louder)

3 I have to *look up* the dates of some famous battles for my history project. (to remember/to check in a reference book)

4 You know he told us he used to be a professional footballer. Well, he *made* it all *up*! (to invent/to tell the truth)

5 If you just *shut up* for a moment and let me explain! (to stop talking/to stop moving)

6 The teacher *told* the pupils *off* for being late for class. (to reprimand/to thank)

2   There is one word missing from each of these sentences. Decide what it is and where it should go.

Example: You need to speak a little so they can hear you at the back.
  You need to speak *up* a little so they can hear you at the back.

1 I wish my dad wouldn't always tell off for being untidy!

2 When you get through David, can you tell him about the party?

3 He was so surprised at what they were saying that he just shut and said nothing.

4 She was a good storyteller and could make wonderful stories about animals.

5 I looked this word in my dictionary but it's not there.

6 She's good at getting a difficult idea very quickly.

3   Complete these sentences. (You don't have to tell the truth if you don't want to!) Compare your sentences with another student.

1 The last time I told someone to shut up was …

2 It took me ages to get through to …

3 I have to remember to speak up when …

4 I remember one teacher used to tell me off for …

5 Once I made up a whole story about …

6 … and so I looked it up in a dictionary.

7 … but I couldn't get across what I meant.

"Yes Charlie—I'm pretty sure she's giving me a cordless telephone."

Writing: discursive composition

1   Read this task. Discuss your opinion of the subject with other students.

2   Read the notes that a student has made below. Which of the points were mentioned in your discussion?

Task

Your class has recently been discussing the idea of studying English at home with a computer. Your teacher has asked you to write a composition summarising the main points of your discussion in 110–130 words.

LEARNING ENGLISH BY COMPUTER

- study in comfort of own home (make coffee, etc.)
- no travelling to school
- no help from other students
- cheaper
- choose when you study
- study the things you want to study
- no correction of my pronunciation

- immediate answers to exercises + explanations
- no discipline of having to study at a certain time each week
- videos of native speakers talking in different situations (can replay)

3   Before you write your answer to the task in Exercise 1, read the composition below. It was written in answer to the question *Is it better to read a book or see the film of that book?* Number these stages in the correct order.

a) the advantages of reading the book ☐
b) summary of opinion ☐
c) introduction to the composition ☐

READ THE BOOK OR SEE THE FILM?

People often discuss whether the book or the film of a story is better. There are different arguments on each side.

Firstly, as far as I'm concerned, when you read the book, you can imagine what the characters and places are like. Your imagination will often be more interesting than what is in a film. Films are also usually only two hours long and it is impossible to tell the story of a normal book in just two hours. In addition, it is difficult to carry a film around with you on the train or on the bus!

There are obviously examples where the film is better than the book. However, I believe that in general it is much better to read the book than to see the film.

4   Look at this sentence. The words in italics are a linking phrase of addition. Find two more in the letter in Exercise 3.

She passed all her exams. *As well as that*, she got the top grade in every subject!

5   Now link these pairs of sentences using the words/phrases from Exercise 4.

Example: My maths teacher is strict. He gives us lots of homework.
*My maths teacher is strict. **As well as that**, he gives us lots of homework!*

1   This book is easy to read. It's got a great ending.
2   We went to lots of great places in Florence. The weather was fantastic.
3   The job was boring. The pay was terrible.
4   His sister is very clever. She's captain of the basketball team.
5   My bedroom is quite big. It's got a great view of the city.

6   Now write your answer to the task in Exercise 1.

1   Use some of the ideas from Exercise 2.
2   Organise the composition logically as in Exercise 3.
3   Include appropriate linking words/phrases of addition.
4   Check you have written the correct number of words (110–130).

▶ Writing reference (Compositions) p. 156

▶ Progress test 3: Teacher's Book

1 Each of the following sentences has a mistake with vocabulary about sports or sounds. Find the incorrect word and replace it with the correct one.

1 I'm so tired. I just can't stop sneezing.

2 I love going to watch the motor chasing on Saturdays.

3 I couldn't hear what she was saying because she was whistling.

4 My bat broke when I was playing tennis with Peter yesterday.

5 Atishoo! Could I have a tissue, please? I've been whispering all day.

6 There's a new net in the park where you can practise running.

7 He's a good leader so they've made him boss of the football team.

8 When you play doubles in tennis, there are four players on the pitch.

9 It's really important that you wear a hat when you're on a motorbike.

10 There were 50,000 competitors watching last week's football match.

11 Please don't crash the door. Can't you close it more quietly?

12 If there is a problem with a point in a tennis match, the leader has the final decision.

2 Choose the correct alternative – A, B or C – to complete each of these sentences.

1 Have you finished the washing-up ....?
   A never   B yet   C just

2 He's walked to school .... he moved here.
   A since   B for   C ever

3 .... your brother played tennis before?
   A Have   B Has   C Does

4 You don't need to phone her. I've .... done it.
   A ever   B since   C already

5 It's my first time in a plane. I've .... flown before.
   A never   B ever   C already

6 Paul left two minutes ago. You've .... missed him.
   A since   B just   C yet

7 Hurry up! I've been in this queue .... hours!
   A for   B since   C already

8 Mia and Josie .... come back from Argentina.
   A just   B has   C have

9 Have you .... seen such a fantastic film!
   A ever   B never   C already

10 Wait! I haven't finished ....!
   A yet   B already   C never

3 Complete these sentences by writing the correct form of the verb in brackets (past simple or present perfect).

1 I work in a shop. I .... (work) in that shop for two years.

2 Sally .... (never, go) to a foreign country.

3 We .... (move) house three weeks ago.

4 Please keep that room tidy. I .... (just, tidy) it.

5 .... (you, ever, see) the Pyramids in Egypt?

6 How long .... (you, learn) the piano, before you stopped?

7 A What about going to see Shrek?
   B No, I .... (already, see) it.

8 I .... (have) this watch since I was a little boy.

9 .... (you, tell) Georgia about the party yet?

10 I .... (go) on the London Eye when I was staying in London.

4 Complete these sentences by choosing the correct alternative.

1 I feel annoyed/annoying when people push to the front of queues.

2 The supermarket was very crowd/crowded. We waited for ages.

3 The nightlife/nightlive in São Paulo is really lively.

4 I'm not going to run marathons again. They are too tired/tiring.

5 You shouldn't drive fast in a build-up/built-up area.

6 I'm amazed/amazing that some people like dangerous sports.

7 London has got a lot of parks and other open zones/open spaces.

8 A lot of people are *frightened/frightening* of going to the dentist.

9 My city is very *polluted/pollution* because there are so many cars.

10 I usually walk to school, because there is so much *traffic/traffics*.

11 The book was so *bored/boring* I didn't finish it.

12 That was the most *embarrassed/embarrassing* experience of my life!

5 **Seven of the following sentences have a mistake in them. Find the mistakes and correct them.**

1 It says in the letter that all students has to register at nine o'clock.

2 You don't have to touch that. It's really hot.

3 I must go to the hairdresser tomorrow. I don't like my hair so long.

4 You can make your own decision. You have to ask me.

5 Must we bring our books to every lesson?

6 During the exam, you mustn't talk to anyone.

7 I don't feel very healthy. I don't have to try to do more exercise.

8 We have to wear a uniform at our school. People wear whatever they like.

9 You have to pass your driving test before you drive on your own.

10 It's a surprise party. You don't have to tell Fiona.

6 **Complete the second sentence in each pair so that it means the same as the first. All these sentences contain a phrasal verb. Write between one and three words.**

1 You will need to speak louder so everyone can hear.
You will need to speak .... so everyone can hear.

2 He got malaria on the second day of his holiday.
He .... with malaria on the second day of his holiday.

3 I can't believe that you invented the whole story.
I can't believe that you made .... the whole story.

4 Quick! Call an ambulance! He's lost consciousness.
Quick! Call an ambulance! He's .... out.

5 I've got too many things to do. It's really making me depressed.
I've got too many things to do. It's really .... me down.

6 When I used that perfume, I got red spots immediately.
When I used that perfume, I .... in red spots immediately.

7 His mother reprimanded him when he stole sweets from his friend.
His mother told him .... when he stole sweets from his friend.

8 I've had enough of listening to you. Will you stop talking now?
I've had enough of listening to you. Will you .... up now?

7 **Complete each sentence with a word from the box. Use each word twice.**

when   where   which   who   whose

1 Oliver, ... I told you about yesterday, wasn't in class today.

2 In August, ... I was on holiday, I met a really nice girl.

3 That's the man .... brother lives next door.

4 Where's the book .... you borrowed from me?

5 The shop .... I used to buy my newspapers has closed down.

6 Do you remember the day .... we first started school?

7 My dad's car, ... was new, has been stolen.

8 Harry, ... bag I've got, is coming round later.

9 I don't like the woman .... shouts a lot.

10 Madrid, ... I was born, is the capital of Spain.

Animal world

Reading 1

1 Look at the photographs and find the names of the animals in the article. (They are all in bold.)

What would life be like if humans had the abilities of other members of the animal kingdom?

Running
A **cheetah** can reach *54 mph* (*86.9 km/h*) in just *2.75 seconds*. It will keep up this top speed for between *183* and *274 metres*.
● If we could do that …
  World *100-metre* record holder Leroy Burrell, who ran the distance in *9.85 seconds* in *1994*, could do it in just 5 seconds.

Jumping
A **flea** can jump *80* times higher than its own body and long jump about *150* times.
● If we could do that …
  We could leap over St Paul's Cathedral, and go *1/4 mile* (*0.4 km*) without touching the ground.

Eating
To understand what serious eating is, we only have to look at the larva of the **American polyphemus moth**. In the first *56 hours* of life it eats *86,000* times its birth weight.
● If we could do that …
  A *7lb* (*3.175 kg*) baby would need *273 tons* of food, that is about *1,087,146* bottles of milk.

Building
Termites in Australia have build mounds up to *20 ft* (*6.096 m*) high.
● If we could do that …
  We'd have skyscrapers four times the height of the Empire State building.

Swimming
A bull **killer whale** was timed in the eastern Pacific in *1958* swimming at *34.5 mph* (*55.5 km/h*). Whales can swim underwater for an hour without coming up for air.
● If we could do that …
  The world's fastest swimmers could cross the Channel (*21 miles* or *34 km*) in less than an hour, swimming underwater all the way.

Thinking
The common **marmoset**'s brain makes up *55.5%* of its entire body weight.
● If we were like that …
  Our head would have to be almost twice its normal size.

2 Read the article and explain the significance of these pictures.

Example: 1 – *We could build this if we could build like termites.*

1

2

3

4

3   Tell another student which statistics you found most surprising.

4   Discuss this question with other students. If you could be an animal, which animal would you be and why?

Example: *I think I'd be a panther because they look good and are dangerous!*

Vocabulary 1: numbers

1

1   Look at all the numbers and measurements (in italics) in the article on page 82. Say if each one refers to a speed, a time, a distance, a year, a weight, a height, a percentage or if it is just an ordinary number.

Example: *54 mph – speed*

2   Try to pronounce the numbers and measurements correctly to a partner. Then listen to the recording and compare.

2   Work with a partner and answer these questions.

1   What years were you both born in?

2   How long can you each hold your breath for?

3   Approximately what percentage of your class are female and what percentage are male?

4   How long do you usually like to sleep at night?

5   Do you know how much you weighed when you were born?

6   What's the fastest speed you've ever travelled at?

7   What's the approximate population of your country?

8   If there are about 1.6 km in one mile, how many miles is your home from where you have your English class?

3   Write down three different numbers which have some meaning for you, e.g. your date of birth. Show another student the numbers. They must say each number and what they think it means.

Example:
Student A *4/8/85.*
Student B *The fourth of August, nineteen eighty five. Is it your date of birth?*

Grammar 1: conditionals (1)

1

1   Match 1–3 to sentences a–f.

1   This sentence describes what always happens.
2   This sentence describes what may possibly happen.
3   This sentence describes something unlikely to happen or hypothetical.

a)   If I were/was a cheetah, I could run at 54 mph.
b)   If we go to the aquarium, we'll see a killer whale.
c)   If you throw a ball for our dog, she always brings it back.
d)   If I arrive late for class, my teacher gets cross.
e)   If you lend him your bike, he'll be really pleased.
f)   If I won the lottery, I would travel round the world.

2   Now look at the names of these different grammatical structures. Match each of them to one of the sentences in Exercise 1.1.

A

Zero conditional: *If* + present simple + present simple

B

1st conditional: *If* + present simple + future form

C

2nd conditional: *If* + past simple + *would, could,* etc.

▶ Grammar reference 10.1 p. 143

2   Think about three things that always happen. Tell another student, using the zero conditional.

Example: If I play a game with *my dad* and he loses, *he gets annoyed*.

1   If I don't get enough sleep at night, ...
2   If I go out with my friend, (*add name*), ...
3   If I am late for my English class, ...
4   If I don't have any lunch, ...
5   If I spend all weekend studying, ...
6   If I eat a big meal late at night, ...

3   Match a clause from column A with a clause from column B to make a 1st conditional sentence.

A

If you do the washing-up,
If you go for a walk,
If you have time,
If you leave now,
If you're hungry,
If you want to come,

B

you can take my umbrella.
you should go on the London Eye.
you'll be very welcome.
we'll stop and get a sandwich.
you'll just catch the last train.
I'll dry.

4   Say if you would do the things in these statements. If not, what would you do instead?

Example: 1 *I wouldn't buy a motorbike, I'd buy a new computer!*

1 If I won £10,000 on the lottery, I would buy a motorbike.

2 If I could introduce one new law, I would make entrance to all cinemas free on Mondays.

3 If I could have a holiday in any country in the world, I would go to the USA.

4 If I could play one musical instrument really well, it would be the guitar.

5 If I could take only one CD (and CD player) to a desert island, it would be *Talking On Corners* by The Corrs.

5   There is a word missing in each of these sentences. Add the missing word.

Example: 1 If they ^do not leave now, they'll be late.

1 If they not leave now, they'll be late.

2 We go travelling if we had the money.

3 You mix the colours blue and red, you get purple.

4 What will you do it rains?

5 If I had more time, I help you fix your bike.

6 If I finish my work, I meet you at the cinema.

7 If I lived near the sea, I go swimming every day.

8 If you don't your homework, our teacher gets annoyed.

6   Read these sentences and decide if each one would most naturally be a zero, 1st or 2nd conditional sentence. Then put the verbs in an appropriate form in each one.

Example: 1 *1st conditional: If you can come to the meal tonight, will you ring me?*

1 If you (*can*) come to the meal tonight, (*you ring*) me?

2 If you (*press*) that button, you (*get*) extra sugar.

3 (*you mind*) if I (*open*) the window?

4 I (*cycle*) to school if it (*be not*) quite so far.

5 If you (*go*) shopping this afternoon, (*you buy*) me a white T-shirt?

6 If I (*know*) his telephone number, I (*phone*) him.

7 I (*give*) you a lift to the party, if I (*get*) back from college in time.

8 If I (*eat*) oysters, I (*feel*) sick!

Use of English: cloze

1   Have you ever had a pet? If so, what was it and how did you feel about it? Can you think of any advantages of having a pet?

Example: *Pets always listen to you!*

2   Read this text. What groups of people does it say have particularly benefited from contact with animals?

Positive pets

Animals in the house help us relax and are good company. In fact, keeping a pet is even good (1) .....*for*...... our health. One study has found that pet ownership was the (2) .... important thing in helping people with heart disease to live longer.

In several countries, including (3) .... United States and Britain, a common therapy for disabled children (4) .... riding. When they ride, these children are on a level with other people, instead (5) .... looking up at them from a wheelchair. In time, learning to control a horse also helps them to control (6) .... own bodies.

Some doctors also encourage dog owners to bring their pets to visit patients (7) .... hospital. The patients can play (8) .... the animals and build up a relationship with them (9) .... part of their treatment. Having another creature to love (10) .... care for gives even the loneliest people a powerful reason for living.

3   Read the text again and complete each space with one word from the box. (There are more words than you need.)

did	with	and	as	their	in	of	up
the	most	its	who	at	is	~~for~~	from

4   Discuss with other students what you think of the ideas in the text.

Example: *I agree that animals in the house help you relax. I always feel better after playing with my cat.*

Speaking: coming to a decision

1   What do you think this photo shows? What do you think you can do there?

2   Listen to two groups of friends trying to decide what to do in the evening. Which of the following possibilities are suggested in each conversation?

Going ...
to see a film   to a nightclub   to a concert
to another friend's house   to the Rainforest Café
to the Hard Rock Café   to a fast food restaurant
for a pizza

3   Listen to the two conversations again. Complete these sentences, which are used to come to a decision. Use the words and phrases in the box.

so let's	right	good idea	so	agree	idea

Conversation 1
Yes, that's a .... I .... Tania and Simon aren't hungry .... go and see a film.

Conversation 2
I think you're .... We're all hungry .... going for a pizza is the best ....!

4

1   Work in groups of four. Look at the transcript for one of the two conversations in Exercise 2 on page 160. Each student should be one of the friends. Read the conversation out loud. Then listen to it on the recording again. Was your pronunciation similar?

2   Have the conversation again. This time, try not to look at the transcript.

5   Work with other students. Plan to do something this evening. At the end of your conversation, make sure you come to a final decision, like this:

1   Express your agreement with the idea, e.g. *Yes, that's a good idea. I agree.*

2   State the reason for the decision, e.g. *Tania and Simon aren't hungry so ...*

3   State the final decision, e.g. *Let's go and see a film.*

Listening

1   Look at the photographs. How does each one make you feel? Choose one of the pictures and say if it reminds you of either a) something that happened to you, b) an animal you know or c) a story you heard about. Tell other students.

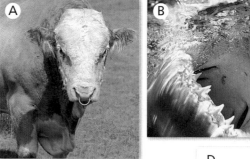

2   Which photograph on page 85 do you think each word in the box is connected to?

a beach	a pond	to scream	fur
camping	a joke	fish	to faint

3   Listen to different people telling stories. Match each story to one of the pictures in Exercise 1.

4   Now answer these questions.

Story 1

1 How far into the water was the speaker when someone cried 'Shark!'?

2 What was the real cause of the panic?

Story 2

1 What is directly outside his dad's study?

2 Why did Twix fall into the pond?

Story 3

1 Where was the speaker when the story happened?

2 What did the speaker nearly do?

Story 4

1 Where was the speaker when the story happened?

2 What saved them from being attacked?

Vocabulary 2: story-telling devices

1   Read the transcripts of the stories you heard in the *Listening* section on page 159. Find examples (in italics) of words or phrases that:

a) are used to show the speaker is very surprised (Stories 1 and 4).

b) are used to get back to the main point of the story (Stories 1, 2, 3 and 4).

c) introduce the last part of the story (Stories 1 and 4).

d) are used to say something happened quickly (Stories 1 and 4).

e) are used for general emphasis (Stories 1 and 2).

f) don't have much meaning but help to link sentences (Stories 1, 2 and 3).

g) introduce the next part of the story (Stories 1 and 2).

Example: e) *Honestly*

2   Complete each of these sentences with an appropriate phrase from the box.

in the end	anyway	honestly
you know	suddenly	can you believe it?

1 Then without warning, Gerry .... stopped the car. I had no idea why.

2 And then – .... – he jumped in the water with all his clothes on!

3 And we had a really nice meal with coffee and everything. ...., as I was saying, she was telling me about her brother who is in India. Apparently, he's not having a very good time.

4 After waiting for nearly an hour for a bus, ... one came along. We were so happy to see it.

5 .... , I don't think I've ever been so surprised in my whole life!

6 Tim was a bit upset when she didn't come with us, ..., he's quite a sensitive guy.

3   Choose one of the stories on page 159. Read it carefully. Then tell it to another student in your own words including some of the words and expressions from Exercise 1.

Reading 2

1   What is the animal in the photo on page 87? Why do you think he might be famous?

2   Read the introductory paragraph in the article (in bold) and check your ideas.

3   Read the complete article quickly to answer this question. (Don't worry about the numbers, spaces and highlighted words.)

Do you get the feeling that Cheetah enjoys his life, or not?

A day in the life of Cheetah

Cheetah, who is 63, is the oldest chimpanzee in captivity and was born in Liberia. He later came to Hollywood where he starred in 50 films, most famously in 18 *Tarzan* titles. At his peak he was earning $500 a day. He now lives in Palm Springs, California with his minder, Dan Westfall, and a number of relatives and friends.

I usually wake between 6 a.m. and 7 a.m. and take a few minutes to have a good stretch. In summer I sleep anywhere cool, but in winter I snuggle down in the newspaper and straw on my sleeping shelf. (1) .... I sit at the table while he cooks some porridge just the way I like it, with water and a bit of sugar.

I spend the morning relaxing in my house which has a TV, radio, air conditioning, a refrigerator and a bathroom. Jeeter (my grandson) is seven and a half and very naughty. He teases Susie (my girlfriend) and spits water at the rest of us. (2) .... We have lunch between 12 and 2 p.m., maybe a peanut-jelly sandwich, a couple of pieces of fruit or a raw onion, and some iced tea.

In the afternoon Dan sometimes takes me out on the back of his Honda scooter. (3) .... I don't know why: it can't be the first time they've seen a man driving a bike. Whenever we stop, people try to come and pat and stroke me. Dan warns them off because on a bad day I can get quite annoyed.

My film career started when Dan's uncle, Tony, was sent by the studios to find suitable chimps. (4) .... I was only a few months old but I guess I had star appeal. He smuggled me in under his jacket. Making the Tarzan films was the chance of a lifetime and I enjoyed working with the stars but I don't miss showbiz. I'm fairly down-to-earth but I do love watching the old videos of myself.

I'm famous for being the oldest chimp in captivity. I don't know what I would have done if I hadn't been a film star. It's been a great life. Recently I started painting. I think I'm not bad. Rude people call my work messy; I prefer the term 'abstract'. (5) .... Dan thinks my paintings are good enough to sell.

After dinner we relax by listening to the radio or flicking through the TV channels. I like cartoons or wildlife programmes. (6) .... Then he brings us a bedtime drink of tea or coffee and maybe gives us some colour magazines. There's nothing I like more than looking through them before I drift off.

4

1 Look at each of the spaces in the article. Look at the sentences before and after them. Think what the content of the missing sentences might be.

Example: 1 – *something that happens early in the morning, possibly connected to sleeping or breakfast*

2 Now look at these sentences and decide where each one goes in the article.

Example: *1 C*

A If there's a documentary on chimps, Dan records it so we can watch it over and over.

B He picked me out of the jungle in Liberia in 1933.

C Dan, my human friend, comes to get me for breakfast.

D Dan adds the date and my signature, but apart from that the work is all my own.

E Usually, it's just a bit of fun and I don't mind, but other times he pushes it too far and I'll put him in his place.

F People in cars seem to stop and stare.

5

1 Read the complete article with the missing sentences in place and check that it makes sense.

2 Compare your answers with another student. Explain which words or phrases helped you decide where to put the missing sentences.

6 Work with other students. Look at the highlighted words in the article. For each one:

- look carefully at the context, i.e. the words before and after

- decide what part of speech it is, i.e. verb, adjective, etc.

- suggest a possible meaning of the word that makes sense

- check your idea in a dictionary.

7 Discuss these questions with other students.

1 Have you see any films about animals? What were they? What were they about?

2 Do you like films about animals? Why?/Why not?

3 Do you think it is right to use animals in films? Why?/Why not?

Grammar 2: conditionals (2)

1

1 Read these sentences.

1 If I'd caught the train, I wouldn't have met her.
2 I don't know what I would have done if I hadn't been a film star.

2 Choose a), b) or c) to make these statements about the 3rd conditional correct.

> **1** The 3rd conditional is used to describe something in the a) past b) present c) future which could have happened, but didn't. It often expresses regret or criticism.
>
> **2** It is formed like this:
> *If* + a) past perfect b) present perfect c) past simple, + *could/would have* + past participle

▶ Grammar reference 10.1 p. 143

2 There is a mistake in each of these sentences. Find it and correct it.

Example: 1 *If I hadn't **eaten** that fish, I wouldn't have been sick.*

1 If I hadn't ate that fish, I wouldn't have been sick.
2 I would have be very happy if my parents had bought me a horse.
3 If he worked harder, he probably could have passed his exams.
4 I would had phoned her if it hadn't been so late.
5 She wouldn't have left him if he haven't spent so much time at the office.
6 Did they have known what to do if you hadn't told them?

7 I couldn't have gone to university if my parents didn't given me some money every year.
8 If he'd got in the team, he would had to go to training sessions three times a week.

3

1 Make the following sentences correct and complete using the 3rd conditional.

Example: 1 *If I had known you were in hospital, I would have visited you.*

1 If I / know / you / be / hospital / I / visit you
2 I / help / them / if / they / ask
3 If I / not go / party / not see / Antonia
4 I / send / you / postcard / if I / have / time
5 If / the / weather / not / be / so bad / we / go / out
6 I / miss / tennis practice / if you / not / wake / me up

2 Listen and check your answers.

4 Write down three decisions you've made in the past. Then write how things might have been different.

Examples:
Decision 1 – *to visit my grandmother last weekend*
If I hadn't visited my grandmother last weekend, I would probably have gone out with friends on Saturday night and played tennis on Sunday morning.

Decision 2 – *to study engineering at university*
If I hadn't studied engineering at university, I would probably have gone to drama school.

Writing: report (1)

1 Reports are often written:

● to summarise the results of surveys
● to present sides of an argument and recommendations.

Look at Writing reference (Reports) on page 157. What three things does it suggest you do when writing reports?

2 Look at the task on page 89 and discuss with other students what reasons there might be for this problem. What possible solutions can you suggest?

Task

There is a growing problem of stray cats and dogs on our streets. You have been asked to write a report on the subject by your local authority. Write your report suggesting some reasons for this problem and recommendations for action using 100–120 words.

3 Look at these notes a student made before she wrote her report. Then read her final report and say how it is different from the notes.

REPORT
1 problem getting worse – need to understand reasons
2 reasons: pets as presents then abandoned – no one to catch stray dogs and cats
3 recommend advertising campaign

Report: The problem of stray cats and dogs

Introduction

The problem of stray cats and dogs is getting worse each year. It is important to understand the reasons for this so that we can take appropriate action.

Reasons for the increase in the problem

Firstly, more and more parents are giving pets as presents to children. The families are not prepared for the hard work involved in looking after an animal and the pet is then abandoned. Secondly, many pet owners do not have their pets neutered*. Consequently, these animals are breeding at a worrying rate.

Recommendations

We suggest that there is an advertising campaign to 1) advise families of what is involved in having a pet and 2) remind them of the importance of having their pets neutered.

neuter: to remove part of the sex organs of an animal so that it cannot reproduce

4 Look at the words in italics in these sentences. They are both linkers of consequence. Find a word with a similar meaning in the report in Exercise 3.

1 Our charity has recently received a large donation. *Therefore*, we will be able to build a new home for abandoned cats and dogs.

2 The children would love a pet *so* why don't we buy them a kitten?

5

1 You have been asked to write a short report for an animal magazine on the most popular and practical pets to keep at home. Ask other students what pets they have now or have had in the past. Also find out which animals they prefer as pets and why.

Name of student	Type of pet, e.g. cat	Comments
Claudia	dog (boxer)	loves dogs because they are so friendly

2 Decide how many paragraphs you are going to have in your report and the purpose of each one. Decide what heading each paragraph should have.

Example:

1 Introduction
2 Pets students have and have had
3 Reasons why particular pets are preferred
4 Recommendations

3 Write your report (100–120 words), summarising your findings. Make recommendations as to the most popular and practical pets to keep at home. Use linkers of consequence where appropriate.

► Unit test 10: Teacher's Book

UNIT 11 Danger!

FIGHTING FIRE
CAROLINE PAUL

Reading

1 Discuss these questions with other students.

1 What jobs do you think the two women in the photographs have?

2 Are there any jobs that you think should only be done by women or only by men?

3 What qualities are needed to be a firefighter? What kinds of things do firefighters have to do? Could you imagine being a firefighter?

2 Work with another student. Before you read the book review below, choose one of these groups of words each. Look in a dictionary to check their meaning.

Student A to sweat, to struggle, to rescue

Student B talent, terror, prejudice

When you have finished, explain the meaning of your words to your partner.

3 Read the review. Did the reviewer like the book a little or a lot?

Fighting FIRE

Review by Angela Lambert

You can see from the photograph on the cover that Caroline Paul is a healthy[1], all-American young woman. She is so beautiful that she could easily be a film star. In fact, she is a firefighter. It is her identical twin sister, Alexandra, who has been
5 an actress since the age of 17. Her best-known TV role was in *Baywatch*, the American TV series about lifeguards. Caroline feels that in some ways she and her sister couldn't be more different. 'It's funny how far apart we can be – ash on my face, make-up on hers.' At the same time, however, maybe their
10 lives are similar in some ways: 'Alexandra rescues people on television while I rescue them in real life[2].'

Fighting Fire is an extraordinary book. It is as exciting as any thriller and describes the dangers[3] and terrors of being a firefighter. At the age of only 25, Caroline became a member of
15 the male-dominated San Francisco Fire Department. When she joined she was one of only seven women among 1,500 firefighters. Why did she do **it**? Somehow Caroline needed to test herself against the power of fire. But, as well as that, she had to deal with the attitude of her male colleagues. Some of them were
20 rude, some threatened[4] her and one or two even put her life in

danger. But over a period of eight years she finally won their respect and admiration. Her oldest enemy apologises for his behaviour when she started out. At that time she was more afraid[5] of her colleagues than the fires she had to fight. Caroline
25 writes about what it's like to go into a burning building. Like her, you sweat under the heavy uniform; you struggle with the weight[6] of the huge water hose; you tremble at the top of 30-metre ladders.

By the end, you understand how it is that every firefighter will
30 risk her or his life to save a helpless child or an alcoholic tramp. As Caroline writes: 'There is something about fire that makes us ask the bigger questions, like: Why am I here on this earth?' It is her talent that in telling the story of her fight against male prejudice and ordinary human fear, she helps each reader to ask
35 these basic questions as well.

Caroline Paul's book tells an inspiring and fascinating story. It must be read.

Fighting Fire by Caroline Paul (Bloomsbury, £12.99)
Verdict: Lively, compelling story of a firefighter ****
40

4   For the questions below, choose the correct answer – A, B, C or D. Where possible, make a note of the lines in the article which justify your answers.

1 Who has been on TV?
   A Caroline
   B Alexandra
   C Both of them
   D Neither of them

2 Caroline thinks she and her sister
   A are completely different.
   B are exactly the same.
   C are similar in some ways.
   D should try to be more similar.

3 What does *it* in line 17 refer to?
   A writing the book *Fighting Fire*
   B dealing with the attitude of her male colleagues
   C becoming a film star
   D joining the San Francisco Fire Department

4 Some of Caroline's male colleagues
   A made her feel welcome when she began.
   B changed their attitude over time.
   C were afraid of her.
   D left the Fire Department because of her.

5 Caroline found the work
   A physically hard.
   B physically quite easy.
   C different to what she imagined.
   D too difficult to do.

6 The reviewer thinks the book
   A should get an award.
   B asks too many questions.
   C is mainly for other firefighters.
   D is extremely interesting.

5   Put the numbered words from the text in the correct form in these sentences. Use a dictionary to help you if necessary.

Example: 1 My mother has always been in very good *health* .

1 My mother has always been in very good
   ....

2 Who is your favourite .... author?

3 Don't buy a motorbike, they're so ....!

4 He made some unpleasant .... but I'm sure he won't carry them out.

5 I have always had a terrible .... of heights.

6 You look very thin. How much do you ....?

6   Discuss the review with other students. Does it make you want to read the book? Why?/Why not?

Grammar 1: making comparisons

1   Complete these sentences with *as, more* or *most*.

1 It was **the** .... **dangerous** thing she had ever done.

2 She was .... **afraid** of her colleagues **than** the fire.

3 She is .... **beautiful as** her sister.

2   Work with other students to complete this table.

Adjective	Comparative	Superlative
A old big	older (than) (2)	(1) .... (the) biggest
B quiet happy boring	quieter (than) (4) .... (5)	(3) .... (the) happiest (the) most boring
C exciting intelligent	more exciting (than) (7)	(6) .... (the) most intelligent
D good bad	better (than) (9)	(8) .... (the) worst

▶ Grammar reference 11.1 p. 143

3   The words in Exercise 2 have been divided into four groups. Answer these questions about them.

Adjectives in group A

1 How many syllables do they have?

2 How do you form their comparatives and superlatives?

Adjectives in group B

3 How many syllables do they have?

4 How do you form comparatives and superlatives of those ending in *y*?

Adjectives in group C

5 How many syllables do they have?

6 How do you form their comparatives and superlatives?

Adjectives in group D

7 Are the comparatives and superlatives formed in a regular or irregular way?

4 There is a mistake in each of these sentences. Find it and correct it.

Example: 1 *I'm not* ^as *tall as Kerry.*

1 I'm not tall as Kerry.

2 This is one of oldest universities in the world.

3 The film was definitely exciting than I thought it would be.

4 You look terrible and your cough sounds worst than it was yesterday.

5 Tina speaks more good French than her sister.

6 My schooldays were certainly not the 'happyest days of my life'!

7 This new armchair is a lot more comfortable our old one.

8 The book certainly isn't good as the film.

9 Is Paul thiner than he was before the holidays?

10 There's nothing boringer than doing homework on a sunny evening.

5 Look at the pictures of twins. Describe any differences you can see between them.

Example: *In Picture C, the young man on the left has a fatter face than his twin.*

6 Work with another student. Tell your partner about one or two very good friends of yours and in what ways you are similar or different.

Example: *My best friend is called Marco. I'm shorter and slimmer than him but in other ways we are the same. For example, we have the same sense of humour.*

Vocabulary 1: describing jobs and qualities

1 Divide the words in the box into two groups.

Group 1 = words describing jobs, e.g. *well-paid*

Group 2 = words describing what you need to be in order to do jobs, e.g. *patient*

brave   patient   well-paid   exciting
good with people   imaginative   dangerous
good with numbers   curious   fit   stressful

2 Work with other students. Ask each other about any of the words which you don't know the meaning or pronunciation of. If nobody in your group knows, check in a dictionary.

3 Match the words in Exercise 1 with the jobs in the box. Do you know any other words you can use to describe these jobs or the people who do them? Compare your ideas with other students. Justify your choices.

> firefighter   actor
> teacher   nurse
> police officer
> accountant
> journalist
> photographer

Example: *I think that being a firefighter would be exciting but dangerous. I think that you need to be fit and brave to be a good firefighter.*

4

1 Work with a partner. Say which of the jobs in Exercise 3 you a) would be interested in doing, b) think you might be good at, and c) would never consider doing. Explain why.

2 Think of one other job that you know. What kind of person do you need to be to do it well?

Use of English:
cloze

1 Read the text and find out what the headline means.

2 Read the text again and see if you can think of a word to go in each space **without** looking at the alternatives in Exercise 3.

FATHER AND SON SURVIVE THREE NIGHTS IN SNOW HOLE

A father and his teenage son were recovering yesterday (1) .....*after*..... spending three days and nights in a tiny snow hole sheltering against snow storms (2) .... the Cairngorm mountains.

John Rawson, 44, and his son David, 16, were (3) .... on Wednesday night only after their shelter was found by a group of climbers. They were then flown to hospital where their hands and feet were put in special bags to (4) .... warm them up. Mr Rawson, an experienced climber, had wanted to (5) .... his son to one of Britain's last wilderness areas (6) .... on Sunday night they suddenly found themselves trapped 4,000 ft above sea level by 122 mph winds and snow storms that reduced visibility to zero.

(7) .... from hospital yesterday, the Rawsons said that they had huddled together for (8) .... and ate snow to survive as the days passed. With temperatures reaching –21°C their hands became so numb that they could not open their (9) .... to get food.

It was only by (10) .... that they were found by a group of climbers on a two-day survival course. The group called for help and Mr Rawson and his son were flown to (11) .... by helicopter.

3 Now choose the correct word for each space from these alternatives.

1 A for	B after	C by	D to
2 A through	B among	C within	D in
3 A rescued	B survived	C brought	D escaped
4 A assist	B make	C help	D encourage
5 A show	B display	C meet	D introduce
6 A but	B and	C because	D so
7 A Speak	B Speaking	C Spoken	D Speech
8 A heating	B climate	C warmth	D temperature
9 A rucksacks	B handbags	C briefcases	D satchels
10 A fortune	B lucky	C chance	D random
11 A security	B safety	C protection	D rescue

Listening

1   Imagine you are going walking in mountains where the weather is unpredictable. Discuss what clothes you should wear and what different things you should take with you.

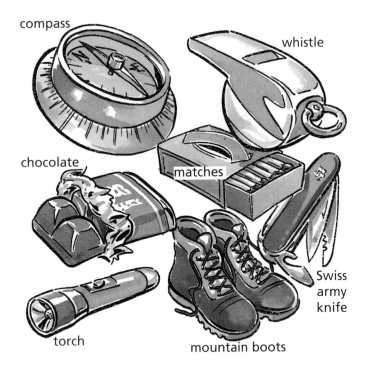

compass
whistle
chocolate
matches
Swiss army knife
torch
mountain boots

2   Listen to the following conversation. Do the two people refer to:

a) one b) two or c) three newspaper articles?

3   Listen to the conversation again and decide if the following statements are true or false.

1 Both people read about the father and son trapped in the mountains.
2 Both people read the article about how to prepare to go up in the mountains.
3 The article suggests wearing three different layers of clothes.
4 The article explains how to get dry if you are wet.
5 The article says it's a good idea to take something which can create heat.
6 The article suggests three different things you can signal with.
7 The article recommends taking food with proteins in.

4   Discuss with other students which of the suggestions from the article were new to you.

Grammar 2: giving advice

1

1 We can use *should*, *shouldn't*, *ought to* and *Why don't you ...?* to give advice. (*Ought to* is less common than the other forms.) Look at these sentences. Which of them advise you to do something? Which advise you not to do something?

1 **You should** prepare properly before you go walking in the mountains.
2 **Why don't you** take a whistle in case you get lost?
3 **You shouldn't** go off on your own.
4 **You ought to** take foods which have a lot of carbohydrates, like bread.

2 Respond to the sentences below with advice. Use *should*, *ought to* or *Why don't you ...?* and the key words in the box.

Example: Your friend wants to lose weight. He doesn't do any exercise.
Why don't you join a gym?

| aspirin + lie down | umbrella | buy |
| gym | cinema | revision |

1 Your friends are going for a walk. You think it's going to rain.
2 You are shopping with a friend. She looks very good in a jacket she is trying on.
3 Your friend is bored and doesn't know what to do tonight.
4 Your friend has a bad headache.
5 Your friend is worried about a school exam.

▶ Grammar reference 11.2 p. 144

2   Think of a problem or situation which is on your mind at the moment. Ask other students for their advice. Decide whose advice you think is best.

Example:
  Student A *I find it difficult to remember new vocabulary.*
  Student B *Why don't you keep a special notebook where you write all the new vocabulary you learn?*
  Student C *You should spend a little time revising new vocabulary after each lesson.*

3 Discuss this question with other students. What is the best piece of advice you've ever been given?

Example: *My uncle told me I should go travelling before going to university. I had a great time!*

Vocabulary 2: survival

1 Match the words (1–10) to the appropriate definition or picture (a–j).

1 to escape

2 an attack

3 poison

4 to signal

5 a bandage

6 blood

7 an injury

8 first aid

9 an earthquake

10 frostbite

a) physical harm that someone gets in an accident or attack

b)

c) when your fingers or toes freeze and are badly damaged

d)

e) simple medical treatment you give quickly to someone who is injured

f)

g) succeed in getting away from an unpleasant place or situation

h) sudden shaking of the Earth's surface

i)

j) violent action that is done to hurt or kill someone

2 Complete the following sentences with the correct form of one of the words in Exercise 1.

1 The nurse put a clean .... on his leg.

2 I'm going on a .... course at the local hospital.

3 The room shook and pictures fell off the walls during the ....

4 I cut my finger and got .... on my shirt.

5 It was so cold they were worried about getting ....

6 He waved to .... that he was ready to start.

7 He was .... by a lion when he was in Africa.

8 Sandy can't play basketball because of a knee ....

9 Factory waste has .... many rivers in this area.

10 He .... from prison by digging a tunnel.

3 Work with another student. Decide how to say each of the sentences in Exercise 2 out loud. Think particularly about the pronunciation of the missing words. Then listen to how they are pronounced on the recording. Was your pronunciation similar?

95

Speaking

1 Discuss with other students what you should do in each of these situations.

1 You are walking in open country with a friend when he is bitten on the foot by a poisonous snake.

2 You are in a friend's house when there is an earthquake.

3 You have been mountain climbing and one of your group has frostbite on his feet.

2 Look at these pieces of advice. Which two pieces of advice go with which situation in Exercise 1?

a) I think you should wash the bite with soap and water as soon as you can.

b) I don't think you should try to rub the skin.

c) I've heard that if you are outside, you ought to move away from buildings.

d) I've been told that you ought to avoid direct heat, like an electric fire.

e) It's important to wrap a bandage tightly above the foot.

f) I read somewhere that it's a good idea to stand in a doorway.

3 Now read the advice on page 160. Which advice did you think of? Which advice did you not think of?

Writing: informal letter (4)

1 Read the task and the letter written by a student below. Has she written about an appropriate subject for this task?

Task

You are writing a letter to an English penfriend. Tell them about a frightening or dramatic experience you had recently (about 120 words).

Dear Monica,

I must apologise for not having responded sooner to your previous letter. Actually I've been really busy with school but I had to write and tell you about what happened to me last week.

It all started when my brother and I went for an early morning swim. We have a favourite place not far from our house. Anyway, we had just got down to the beach when I thought I could hear someone shouting. I looked out to sea and there was someone waving and shouting. It was a young man who was swimming by himself – he'd got cramp and couldn't swim back. My brother and I found the branch of a tree on the beach, ran to the water and swam out. We held the branch out for the young man to grab hold of, then we pulled him back to the beach. He was very grateful and invited us both to his family's house for dinner. I'm really glad we were able to help!

How are you? Please write in the near future and inform me about what is happening in your life.

Yours faithfully,

Jenny

2   Read Jenny's letter again and number these pictures in the correct order.

A

B

C

D

3   Read Jenny's letter again and answer these questions.

1 Is the letter divided into appropriate paragraphs?

2 Which parts of the first and last paragraphs are not written in an appropriate style? Can you correct them?

3 The letter is too long. How much needs to be cut to reduce it to the right length? How could you do this? For example, what details could you leave out of the second paragraph?

▶ Writing reference (Paragraphs) p. 149 and (Formal and informal language) p. 151

4   Now write your own answer to the task in Exercise 1. If necessary, refer to the pictures opposite.

1 Brainstorm ideas.

2 Make notes.

3 Divide your letter into separate paragraphs.

4 Use informal language.

▶ Writing reference (Planning your writing) p. 152

▶ Unit test 11: Teacher's Book

Do you remember?

Reading

1 What things do you find easy to remember? What things do you find difficult to remember? Think about:

- names of people
- dates in the past
- events in your early childhood
- dreams
- stories of books or films
- friends' birthdays
- phone numbers.

2 Read the article quickly. What kinds of things does John have problems remembering? (Don't worry about the missing sentences.)

3

1 You are going to put the six missing sentences in the correct place in the article. Before you do this, find the first space. Read the sentence before it and the sentence after it. Then decide if these statements are true or false.

1 The missing sentence probably refers to your view of John.
2 The missing sentence probably refers to the night after the party.
3 The missing sentence probably refers to John's girlfriend.

2 Now decide which of the sentences below is missing from the first space.

A On the other hand, his factual memory is good.
B This is because on one occasion he got a job on a building site and another in a glass factory, which could have had serious consequences.
C If you bumped into him again the following night, however, you might change your opinion.
D When you ask John how he feels about his life, he has quite a down-to-earth attitude.
E However, this is another big problem.
F 'How can I ask someone how their holiday was if I don't remember they had one?' he asks.

4 Read the complete article again. Choose the most suitable sentence from the list A–F above for each space (1–6) in the article. Underline or highlight the words/phrases that helped you decide. (Three have been done for you already.)

the man with no past

If you met John Forbes at a party, you would probably think he was a shy but good-natured 21-year-old. If you started talking about one of his favourite subjects – politics, science fiction or computer games – you would find him likeable and amusing. (1) .... For a start, he wouldn't recognise you and he certainly wouldn't remember your name or the conversation from the previous night.

John isn't rude or arrogant; he just cannot remember. His problem is that he suffers from a rare brain disorder that stops him remembering everyday events. (2).............

In John's world there is no past or future. He has difficulty remembering a telephone conversation from a moment earlier. He needs constant reminders about appointments and meal times. He cannot find his way around town and rarely goes to places he doesn't know. If he does, he takes a map, detailed notes of the route and the reason for the journey. (3) .... He was successful at school and can remember history dates and even complete passages from his favourite films. He knows the names of the important members of the government but then cannot remember that his sister, Kate, left college a year ago.

John would like to lead a normal life, which means getting a job and learning to drive for example. (4) .... Not because he couldn't learn the road signs, but because he might see a warning sign, forget it, and fail to take the necessary action.

As for work, his parents used to be very keen for him to get a job. They even allowed him to sign up with employment agencies without mentioning his memory problems. They would not allow it now. (5) .... 'If you don't remember being told to keep your hand away from a piece of machinery, you might get it chopped off,' says his father, Mike.

John spends a lot of his time at home, playing computer games and watching TV news reports at regular intervals so he can remember the information. (6) .... As he says, 'Memory is a major factor in what makes you and gives you your beliefs. I live for the moment – I don't think about tomorrow.'

5 Discuss your answers to Exercise 4 with a partner. Explain which words and phrases helped you decide which sentence to put in each space.

6 What do you think is the worst thing about John's situation?

Grammar 1: *can, could, be able*

1 Read the sentences underneath the pictures and decide if these statements are true or false.

1 *Can* and *could* are used to talk about ability. They are also used to make requests. (In requests, *could* is more polite and formal than *can*.)

2 With *can* and *could*, questions and negatives are made with *do*.

3 We usually use *was/were able* to say that somebody managed to do something that was not easy.

A *He can remember history dates.*

B *He couldn't learn the road signs.*

C *Can I borrow your bike?*

D *I was able to open the window with difficulty.*

▶ Grammar reference 12.1 p. 144

Watch Out *able to* or *could?*

Which alternative is more appropriate in each sentence?

Which alternative means something is generally true?

Which alternative means something is possible on one particular occasion?

1 The box was very heavy but I *was able to/could* lift it.

2 I *was able to/could* run quite fast when I was younger.

2 Complete these sentences with *can/can't* or *could/couldn't* and one of the verbs in the box.

Example: 1 *can speak*

hear	swim	answer	speak	see
	do	come	go	

1 I .... a little Arabic but I can't read it.

2 .... you .... to my party on Saturday?

3 I .... to work yesterday. I wasn't feeling very well.

4 It's a lovely hotel. We .... the sea from our bedroom window.

5 She loves water. She .... by the time she was five.

6 I .... you very well. Please speak up a bit.

7 When we were children, we .... usually .... what we wanted.

8 The exam was difficult. I .... a lot of the questions.

3 Answer these questions with *was(n't)/were(n't) able to*. Use the words in brackets.

Example: 1 *We were able to find the way with a good road map!*

1 How did you get here so soon? (*find the way/a good road map*)

2 What happened when the fire broke out? (*escape/bedroom window*)

3 How did you finish your report so quickly? (*use/friend's computer*)

4 Why is Sonia upset? (*get tickets/the Madonna pop concert*)

5 Why do you look so tired? (*get to sleep/last night*)

6 How did they rescue the girl from the river? (*throw/lifebelt*)

4   Tell a partner three interesting things you can do. Decide who can do the most interesting thing.

Example: *I can touch my nose with my tongue. I can speak a little Arabic. I can stand on my hands.*

5   Make a note of any things you could do better when you were younger than you can do now. Then tell another student.

Example: *When I was younger I could swim really well but I'm not very fit now. I could also stand on my head!*

6   Work with a partner. Student A makes a request. Student B gives a reason why it's not possible.

Example:
Student A *Could you open the window, please?*
Student B *No, I'm sorry, I can't. It's locked.*

'Could I see the milk list?'

Vocabulary 1: memory

1   Match the words in the box with the definitions.

> memory   memorise   remind   reminder
> remember   forget   forgetful   unforgettable

1   to have in your mind people, places and events from the past
2   to learn facts, numbers, etc. so that you can remember them later
3   to tell someone about something they must do
4   your ability to remember things
5   to not remember something
6   often forgetting things
7   something that affects you so strongly that you will never forget it
8   a spoken or written message to help you remember something that you might forget

> **Watch Out** *forget*
>
> Which one of these is not possible? Why?
> 1   I've forgotten my keys.
> 2   I've forgotten my keys at home.
> 3   I've left my keys at home.

2   Complete each sentence with one of the words from Exercise 1.

1   The dentist has sent me a .... that I need a check-up soon.
2   Seeing the pyramids in the desert was a completely .... experience.
3   Sssh! I'm trying to .... these dates for my history exam tomorrow.
4   Grandad is getting very .... these days. He's always losing his glasses, for example.
5   I mustn't .... to pick Josie up from school at lunchtime. She finishes early today.
6   He's always had a photographic .... You show him a list of telephone numbers for a few seconds and he can remember them all!
7   Do you .... our French teacher at school. He was bald but he had a big grey beard.
8   When we go shopping, can you .... me to get some batteries for my camera?

3   Discuss these questions with other students.

1   Do you think you have a good, bad or average memory? Why?

2   What different things have you had to memorise in the past?

3   Who is the most forgetful person you know? Give examples of what they forget.

4   Describe one of the most unforgettable experiences you have ever had.

5   Do you ever get sent reminders? Who from? What are they about?

6   What's the last important thing that you forgot to do?

Use of English: error correction

1   Read the text quickly. Then tell another student if there was anything in it which was new information or a new idea for you.

2

1   You are going to read the text again and look for an extra and unnecessary word in each line.

The extra words are all grammar words. They may include:

- prepositions (*in*, *on*, *at*, etc.)
- articles (*the*, *a*, *an*)
- pronouns (*it*, *that*, *what*, etc.)
- auxiliary verbs (*do*, *will*, *am*, etc.)
- determiners (*some*, *much*, etc.)
- parts of comparatives (*more*, *most*, etc.)

Look at line 1. Underline any words in it that may be extra and unnecessary. Read the line, imagining each of the words in turn is not there. Does it still make sense?

2   Compare your ideas with another student. Do you agree?

3   Now read the complete text sentence by sentence. Make a note of the word in each line which is extra. Compare your answers with another student. If there are any differences, discuss why.

The art of forgetting

1   It's amazing what we can to remember and what we forget!

2   Six years after that the death of Princess Diana, a famous

3   magazine reported us that every one of the famous people they

4   had been asked could remember the exact details of how they first

5   heard the news of the princess's whose death on August 31, 1997.

6   We remember such shocking and dramatic events more better

7   than any others but why do we forget with anything? The things

8   we are most often forget are names (of things as well as people),

9   numbers, dates, and a things we do not understand. We also find it

10   hard up to remember anything when we are embarrassed,

11   frustrated, ill or very tired. However this, forgetting happens to us

12   in constantly, and it is perfectly normal. There is, it seems, a limit

13   to what if we can remember. If we could remember everything, all

14   the time, the life would become impossible! As we get older,

15   we lose more and more of memories, leaving only the most

16   important in to the mental space available.

Listening

1   What is your earliest childhood memory? Tell other students about it.

2

1   Listen to someone talking about a childhood memory. Which of the subjects below are they talking about?

   A going to a park
   B holidays by the sea
   C playing with their older brother
   D Christmas
   E their mother's cooking

2   Now read the transcript on page 160. Is your original answer correct? Which words or phrases in the transcript confirm your answer? (Two words have been highlighted for you.)

3   You will hear three more people talking about childhood memories. For each person, choose which of the subjects in the list A–E in Exercise 2 they are talking about. Use the letters only once. There is one extra letter which you do not need to use.

4   Listen to all four extracts again. Then, say how each picture relates to what the speakers said. Check that you know the meaning of the words in the box before you start.

> to pack a suitcase
> to greet
> a mixing bowl
> to decorate
> presents
> to tickle someone

Example: A *This shows the first speaker when she was a child. She is packing her suitcase before going on holiday with her family.*

A

B

C

D

E

F

G

H

Grammar 2: *used to*

1   Look at the illustration below. Does *used to* refer to:

a) a past habit or state?

b) a present habit or state?

I used to love swimming in the sea when I was younger. I didn't use to feel the cold at all!

► Grammar reference 12.2 p. 144

2   There are three mistakes connected with *used to* in this dialogue. Find them and correct them.

A: So, what did you use to be like when you were at school?

B: Oh terrible. I use to be really cheeky to the teachers and I never used to do my homework on time.

A: Did they used to get cross with you?

B: Yes, and once the headmaster asked for my parents to go to the school to see him. It was so embarrassing. I also used to hate getting my annual report from school. My parents used to being very upset when I didn't do well in my school exams.

A: Were they surprised when you told them what job you wanted to do?

B: Yes. They couldn't believe I wanted to be a teacher!

3   Answer the following questions with *Yes* or *No*.

When you were younger, did you use to:

1 have a best friend?

2 go on holiday to the same place every year with your family?

3 get on well with your brothers and sisters?

4 be naughty?

5 enjoy school?

6 have a favourite TV programme?

7 have a special hiding place?

4   Ask another student the questions in Exercise 3. Then ask further questions about the ones they answer *Yes* to.

Example:

Student A *When you were younger, did you use to have a best friend?*

Student B *Yes.*

Student A *What was his or her name?*

Student B *Sylvia.*

Student A *How did you know her?*

Student B *We were at primary school together.*

Student A *Are you still in touch?*

Student B *No, unfortunately not. The last time I saw her was when we left primary school.*

Vocabulary 2: prefixes

1   Look at the words in bold in these sentences. Why do we use the underlined prefixes?

1 Why are there so many <u>ir</u>regular verbs in English?

2 I'm afraid that more than half of your answers were <u>in</u>correct.

3 I used to <u>un</u>pack my case as soon as I arrived at the hotel.

4 I was very <u>im</u>patient for dinner to be ready.

5 Why do you <u>dis</u>agree with everything I say?

6 Isn't it <u>il</u>legal to talk on your mobile phone while you're driving?

2   Which of the prefixes in Exercise 1 go with the words in this box?

> happy   like   possible   legible   friendly
> lock   polite   visible   employed
> honest   responsible

Example: *happy – unhappy*

3   Use the positive or negative form of the words from Exercises 1 and 2 to complete these sentences.

1 Your writing is completely .... I can't read a word of it!

2 These harmful bacteria are actually .... to the human eye.

3 I couldn't .... more. You're completely right that we shouldn't have to do homework in the holidays.

4 I'm sorry but it's .... There is no way that I can be at your house by 6 p.m.

5 Could you .... the front door for me? I'm afraid I haven't got my key.

6 My little brother is very .... He always remembers to say *please* and *thank you*.

7 It is very .... of you to suggest that smoking is trendy! It's important that we discourage young people from smoking.

8 I really .... the way he dominates conversations. When he's around no one else gets a chance to say anything.

Speaking

1   Look at the photographs and discuss these questions with a partner.

1 Where do you think they were taken?

2 When do you think they were taken?

3 Who are the people?

4 How do you think they feel about the situation?

2   Before you describe the photographs, check that you know the meaning of the words in the box. Which words relate to photograph A and which to photograph B?

> a beach   to ride   sand
> the sea   grass   a donkey
> to sit   to chat   a picnic
> a bucket   relaxed
> a sandcastle

3   Take turns with a partner to compare the two photographs. Use some of the vocabulary from Exercise 2. Point out any similarities or differences you noticed in Exercise 1. Speak for at least one minute.

4   Now, listen to someone talking about one of the photographs. Why is it special to them?

5   Choose 1 or 2 below.

1 Do either of the photos remind you of anything in your past? Tell another student.

   Example: *Picture B reminds me of holidays that I used to have with my family. We always used to go to …*

2 Work in groups. Show the other students a favourite photo of yours. Tell them when it was taken, where it was taken and why it is special for you. (If you can't show them a photo, describe a favourite photo from memory.)

A

B

Writing: story (4)

1

1 Read this task and one student's answer.

Task

You have been asked to write a story (in about 100 words) for a student magazine beginning with these words:

I woke up knowing that it was a special day.

2 Now answer the following questions about the student's answer.

1 Is it organised into appropriate paragraphs?
2 Is there appropriate punctuation?
3 Do you notice any spelling mistakes?
4 Is there a good range of vocabulary? Give examples.
5 Are there linking words, e.g *then*, *finally*, *although*? Give examples.
6 Does the writer try to make the story interesting? How?
7 Is it about the right length?

▶ Writing reference (Stories) p. 155

2 Put the words in the box into pairs with similar meaning.

> eventually   as a result   firstly
> just then   at that moment   finally
> so   to begin with

Watch Out *at the end* or *in the end*?

Which phrase in bold means *after a lot of time or discussion*?

1 **At the end** of the film they all went home.
2 **In the end** we decided to forget the bus and walk home instead.

I woke up knowing that it was a special day. It was my 16th birthday. I felt quite exited. Then I heard the post arrive. I ran downstairs to collect all my cards but there weren't any. I was really fed up.

I spent the rest of the day waiting for the phone to ring. I couldn't understand why all my friends had forgoten my birthday. Eventually, my parents suggested going out to see a film. I couldn't think of enything better to do so I agreed.

On the way to the cinema, my dad suddenly stoped in front of a smart nightclub. It looked all dark but as we went inside, suddenly the lights came on. I heard lots of people shouting 'Happy Birthday!' In front of me I could see all my friends standing there in party hats. In the middle of them there was an enormus birthday cake. It was an incredible suprise!

---

3 Now choose the correct alternative in each of these sentences.

1 We took the wrong turning several times and the traffic was terrible but *eventually/as a result* we found their house.

2 We were just looking forward to an evening of peace and quiet but *so/just then* the doorbell rang.

3 *To begin with/At that moment* I think we should see our room. Then, I'd like to explore the town.

4 Unfortunately it started to pour with rain *so/finally* we decided to stay indoors.

5 *Eventually/Firstly*, I'd like to say how pleased I am to be here.

4 Look again at the task in Exercise 1 and follow this procedure.

1 Read the task carefully.
2 Decide what you are going to write about.
3 Make notes of what each paragraph will be about.
4 Write your story. Think about the questions in Exercise 1.2

▶ Writing reference (Editing your writing) p. 153

▶ Progress test 4: Teacher's Book

1 Choose the correct alternative – A, B, C or D – to complete each of these sentences.

1 She gave a .... that they were ready to start.
  A signal B show C move D flag

2 ...., I've never been so embarrassed in my whole life!
  A Suddenly B Honestly C Faithfully
  D Considerably

3 In the ...., we decided to call a taxi.
  A final B conclusion C eventually D end

4 You have to be very .... to be a novelist.
  A imaginative B thinking C knowing
  D mental

5 My job is quite .... at the moment. I have a big report to write.
  A anxious B worried C stressful D worn

6 He had quite a bad .... from playing football.
  A illness B hurt C unconscious D injury

7 My granddad is getting very .... these days.
  A forgetful B forgettable C forgotten
  D forgetting

8 I have to .... all these history dates before tomorrow.
  A memory B remind C memorise D reminder

2 Unjumble the words connected with jobs, survival and memory in these sentences.

1 I always wanted to be a *usern* but I hate the sight of blood!

2 You have to be very *enittap* to be a good teacher.

3 Police officers can quite often be in *aednrg*.

4 You'd be a good *rctoa*. You're very good at different accents!

5 There's been a small *keeqaarhtu* in San Francisco but no one was hurt.

6 I put down some rat *nioosp* but it doesn't seem to have worked.

7 It was really freezing but my gloves stopped me getting *ttefiosrb*!

8 The nurse will change your *gaadneb* every day.

9 Don't *rtgefo* to pick me up at 7 p.m. We mustn't be late.

10 I have a terrible *ymmroe* for names these days. I must be getting old.

3 In each of the following pairs of sentences, complete the second sentence with 1–3 words so that it has the same meaning as the first sentence.

1 a) Last night she looked sadder than she does now.
  b) She doesn't look .... she did last night.

2 a) It's a good idea to take a torch with you.
  b) You .... to take a torch with you.

3 a) You haven't said a more intelligent thing all day!
  b) That's .... intelligent thing you've said all day!

4 a) I always visited my grandmother on Sunday mornings.
  b) I always .... to visit my grandmother on Sunday mornings.

5 a) Nobody in the team plays as well as he does.
  b) He's .... player in the team.

6 a) You should go out more and have some fun.
  b) Why .... go out more and have some fun?

7 a) Her last CD was better than her new one.
  b) Her new CD isn't as .... last one.

8 a) I knew how to juggle when I was quite young.
  b) I was .... to juggle when I was quite young.

4 Write these numbers as words.

Example: 25 – *twenty-five*

1 37 ....

2 149 ....

3 6,963 ....

4 73,000 ....

5 1/4 ....

6 98 ....

7 5.96 ....

8 12,054 ....

5 Use the word given in capitals at the end of each sentence to form a word that fits in the space.

1 I went swimming with dolphins this summer. It was an .... experience! **FORGET**

2 He sent her a .... about the meeting with the sales director. **REMIND**

3 If I .... all the irregular verbs, I should do well in the test. **MEMORY**

4 His writing is .... I can never make any sense of it. **LEGIBLE**

5 Don't be so .... The train will be here soon. **PATIENT**

6 Could you .... the front door and let me in, please? **LOCK**

7 He's been .... for six months now. He's quite depressed about it. **EMPLOY**

8 That dog is .... He attacked the postman yesterday. **DANGER**

9 She's got an incredible .... She thinks of the most amazing stories. **IMAGINE**

10 The .... from this snake can kill a human being. **POISONOUS**

6 Decide if these sentences are grammatically correct or not. If not, correct the mistakes.

1 He was finally able move the wardrobe with the help of his brother.
....

2 My parents used to always read me a story before I went to sleep.
....

3 Why don't you taking some waterproof clothes in case it starts to rain.
....

4 They couldn't decide whether to turn left or right.
....

5 She didn't use to playing any sport when she was younger.
....

6 This new game is the more exciting than the last one you bought me.
....

7 You should to have a holiday. You're working too hard.
....

8 He's not as good at volleyball as he says he is.
....

7 Choose the correct alternative in each of these sentences.

1 If you *drop/dropped* the box, I will be very cross.

2 If you *had/had had* the money, which of these jackets would you buy?

3 If you *press/pressed* this button you get sugar in your coffee.

4 If you *asked/had asked* me I would have lent you my bike.

5 If he sees you he always *will say/says* 'Hello'.

6 If you hadn't been so rude, they *will/would have* let us stay.

7 If he got up earlier, he *would get/would have got* to school on time.

8 If you phone me, I'*ll come/come* and pick you up.

UNIT
13 Down under

Reading 1

1 Describe what you can see in these pictures. What is the connection between them?

2 When you read a text in English, try to predict the content from the title and any pictures that are with it. This will make it easier to understand. This text is about Australia. Discuss what you know about Australia with other students and make a list.

Example:
> **Student A** *Well, Canberra is the capital of Australia.*
> **Student B** *And Crocodile Dundee is one of my favourite films. That's Australian.*

3 Now read the text (2–3 minutes only) to answer this question: What is the writer's attitude to Australia? Does he feel

a) uninterested in it?

b) neutral about it?

c) impressed by it?

Be prepared to justify your answer by referring to words or phrases in the text. (Do **not** worry about words you do not know.)

4 Which one of the pictures is not mentioned in the text? Which part of the text does each of the other pictures refer to?

Example: *Picture E refers to Paragraph 3 where it says the Aborigines invented ocean-going transport.*

Down under

1 Australia is the world's sixth largest country and its largest island. It is the only island that is also a continent, and the only continent that is also a country. It is also the only country that began as a prison.

2 As well as all that, Australia is the home of the largest living thing on Earth, the Great
5 Barrier Reef, and of the famous Ayers Rock (or *Uluru*, to use its Aboriginal name). It has more things that will kill you than anywhere else. All of the world's ten most poisonous snakes are Australian. You may also be eaten by sharks or crocodiles, carried out to sea by strong currents, or left to die in the baking outback. It's a hard place.

3 And it is old. Perhaps 45,000 years ago, perhaps 60,000, it was quietly invaded by the
10 Aborigines. Amazingly, it also seems that they could only get there by inventing ocean-going transport – at least 30,000 years before anyone else.

4 This is so extraordinary that most history books only give it one or two paragraphs. They then move on to the second invasion – the one that begins with the arrival of Captain James Cook and *HMS Endeavour* in Botany Bay in 1770. Apparently, it's not important
15 that Captain Cook didn't discover Australia and that he wasn't even a captain when he arrived. For most people, including most Australians, this is where the story begins.

5 The world those first Englishmen found was different to anything they had seen before. Its seasons were back to front and its constellations were upside down. Add to that, the strange animals they found there. The most typical of them didn't run but *bounced* across
20 the landscape, like balls. The continent was full of unusual life. There was a fish that could climb trees; a fox that flew (it was actually a very large bat); crustaceans so big that a grown man could climb inside their shells.

6 In short, there was no place in the world like it. There still isn't.

5   Read the text again. For each question, decide if A, B, C or D is the best answer.

1 Australia is
  A an island and a country but not a continent.
  B an island, a country and a continent.
  C a country and a continent but not an island.
  D a continent and an island but not a country.

2 How many different ways does the writer say you can die in Australia?
  A one
  B two
  C three
  D four or more

3 Why is it surprising that the Aborigines came to Australia?
  A Because it is such a dangerous place.
  B Because it means they were technologically far ahead of other races.
  C Because they had nothing in common with the people living there.
  D Because they had no maps.

4 Which of these points does the writer make?
  A Most people think the story of Australia begins in 1770.
  B James Cook discovered Australia.
  C Cook was made a captain when he arrived in Australia.
  D Most history books don't mention the arrival of the Aborigines.

5 What did the first Englishmen notice about Australia?
  A how different to their home it was
  B how many animals there were
  C how terrible the weather was
  D how strangely the people behaved

6 Where does this text come from?
  A an encyclopaedia
  B a letter to a friend from someone on holiday in Australia
  C a book by a visitor to Australia
  D a history book

6   Find these words in the text. Look at words and sentences that come before and after. Then look at the suggested meanings below. One of the meanings is not correct. Which is it? What do you think this word actually means?

1 *current* (l.8): continuous movement of water in a particular direction

2 *to invade* (l.9): enter a country using military force in order to take control

3 *constellation* (l.18): group of stars

4 *crustacean* (l.21): a type of animal with fur, for example rabbit, fox, koala

7   Discuss these questions with other students.

1 How does this text make you feel about Australia?
2 Does it make you want to read more about it? Why?/Why not?
3 Does it make you want to go there?

Vocabulary 1: the physical world

1   Work with other students. Name one more example of each place in the table.

Place		Example
continent		Africa
country		Brazil
island		Crete
ocean		the Atlantic
lake		Lake Titicaca
river		the Nile
mountain		Mount Everest
forest		the Black Forest
desert		the Sahara

Watch Out *desert* or *dessert?*

Choose the correct spelling for the words in italics in each sentence below. Where is the main stress in each of the words?

1 They had enough water for three days in the *desert/dessert*.

2 He ordered some ice-cream for *desert/dessert*.

2 Check the pronunciation of the words in Exercise 1 in an English–English dictionary. Try saying them to another student. Then listen to the pronunciation on the recording. How accurate was your pronunciation?

3 Work with other students. Read these sentences. Decide if you think each one is true or false. See how many your group can get right.

1 Mountains are formed in many different ways.

2 The continents we live on are slowly moving.

3 The longest mountain range in the world is under water.

4 The Volga is the longest river in Europe.

5 The Mediterranean was once a desert.

6 In 1963 a new island rose out of the sea.

7 Ocean waves can travel as fast as a jet plane.

8 If you sailed directly south from Iceland, you would sail for thousands of miles before reaching land.

9 If all the glaciers melted, London, New York and Paris would be drowned.

4 Work with a partner. Student A look at the drawing of island A on page 159. Student B look at the drawing of island B on page 160. Take turns to describe your islands. When you listen to your partner's description, try to draw the island. Use the symbols from Exercise 1.

Example:

Student A *In the north of my island, there are some mountains. Then, in the north-west, there is …*

Grammar 1: *like*

1 Match these uses of *like* to the correct examples, 1, 2 and 3.

A
like + *-ing*. This is used to talk about what you enjoy doing.

B
would like + infinitive. This is used to ask for or offer something in a polite way.

C
like (preposition). This is used before a noun or a pronoun. It means something is similar to something else.

1 *I'd like an ice-cream.*

2 *I like skiing.*

3 *I'm like my dad.*

2 Put the words in these sentences in the correct order.

1 to Australia like would visit you?

2 sister say am like people my that I exactly

3 Ayers Rock would to she see like

4 early like don't the I getting morning up in

5 tonight like would do what you to?

6 shop jacket one this like the is last in the

7 friends weekend out she her likes going the at with

8 class last this like not one was is the I year in

9 computer homework doing do the you on like your?

3 Read this dialogue. Expand the sentences so they are grammatically complete and correct.

Example: *Fiona* OK, so what would everyone like to do this evening?

Fiona OK, so what / everyone like / do / this evening?

Sam Oh, I don't know. I / quite like / go bowling. We / not go / ages!

Jim I / prefer / do something else. I / hurt / leg. Anyway, I never / like go / bowling. It / be / always / too crowded and noisy.

Fiona How about you Zoe?

Zoe I / feel / like Jim. / I / like / have / quiet evening. How about / get / video and go back / my place?

4 Discuss these questions with other students.

1 If you could go for a two-week holiday anywhere in the world (all expenses paid), where would you like to go, and why?

2 Which person in your family are you most like? In what ways are you like them?

3 What do you like doing on Sunday mornings?

Listening 1

1 Look at the notes below about visiting Sydney. Some information is missing. You will hear a tour guide talking to a group of tourists who will be in Sydney for the next two days. For each question, fill in the missing information in the numbered space.

VISITING SYDNEY (PROGRAMME OF EVENTS)

This evening:

(1) *Barbecue.* with harbour view.

Then, performance by two top (2) ....

Tomorrow:

Breakfast from (3) ....

Meet in reception at (4) ....

Morning activity: tour of 'The Rocks' (many old buildings, art galleries and (5) ....).

Afternoon activity: (6) .... with Daniel or scenic ride on the Manly (7) ....

Evening activity: visit Sydney Opera House or (8) .... (well-known nightclub).

2 Discuss these questions with other students.

1 Are these the kind of holiday activities you would enjoy? Why?/Why not?

2 Who in your family might enjoy them?

Vocabulary 2: tourism

1 The questions on the left are all connected to the subject of holidays and tourism. Match each one to its answer on the right.

Questions

1 Was it a long flight?

2 Did you buy anything in duty-free?

3 What did you think of London?

4 Have you taken many photos?

5 How did you get here from the airport?

6 Would you like to do a bit of sightseeing today?

7 Are you going to buy a guidebook?

8 Have you bought many souvenirs?

9 Did you have a look round the shops?

Answers

a) Yes, but not for long. They were very crowded.

b) Yes, lots. Four or five films. Now I need to get them developed!

c) On the Underground.

d) About three hours. Not too bad.

e) That would be great. Why don't we go and see Buckingham Palace?

f) It's a great place. It's got some amazing museums and the nightlife is fantastic!

g) No, I don't need to. My dad's already given me one.

h) Just a camera. But it was really cheap!

i) Just one or two, as presents for my family.

2 Now write one alternative answer to each of the questions in Exercise 1.

3

1 Look at the questions in Exercise 1 again. Think about how you might say them. Which word(s) should have the main stress? (Main stress is usually on the most important word in the sentence.)

Example: *Was it a **long** flight?*

 2 Listen to the recording and compare your ideas.

4 Work with a partner. Either a) Describe a real holiday you have had or b) Imagine a fantastic holiday you have just had.

1 Decide where you went and how long for.

2 Make notes about some of the things you did.

3 Be prepared to answer some of the questions in Exercise 1 about your holiday.

5 Work with a different partner. Ask about his/her holiday. (Use some of the questions from Exercise 1 if you can, but use other questions of your own as well.)

Example:

Student A *So, tell me first, where did you go on holiday?*

Student B *Well, I had this amazing holiday in Mexico!*

6 Finally, tell the partner you worked with in Exercise 4 about the holiday you have just heard about it. Was it more interesting than yours?

Example: *The holiday I found out about was in Mexico. It sounded great! First, they ...*

Speaking

1 Listen to a student (Claudia) comparing and contrasting the photographs below. Which of these things does she talk about?

1 what the people may be doing

2 where they might come from

3 where they may be now

4 how much money they have

5 how they might be feeling

6 what they might do the next day

7 how she feels about holidays like these

2

1 Look at the transcript. The missing words can help you describe different photographs. Which words do you think are missing?

Well, both pictures (1) .... young people on holiday maybe and travelling, but in very different ways! In picture A I can (2) .... two young people carrying, what's the word, oh yes, rucksacks. They look (3) .... they're in the middle of a city. The buildings (4) .... me of Spain or Italy but I'm not sure. On the (5) .... hand, picture B seems to be in the country.

The first couple probably don't have much money (6) .... the people in picture B must be quite well off because the car (7) .... quite expensive! Also, the people in the second picture look quite relaxed but the first couple look hot and tired as (8) .... they've been walking around for a long time. I think they (9) .... be looking for somewhere to stay.

2 Listen again and check your ideas.

3   Now work with another student. Look at the two photographs below and decide which words and phrases in the box will be useful to talk about picture A, picture B or both.

> outdoors   a museum guide   to listen   a group   grass
> an exhibition   to explain   a coach

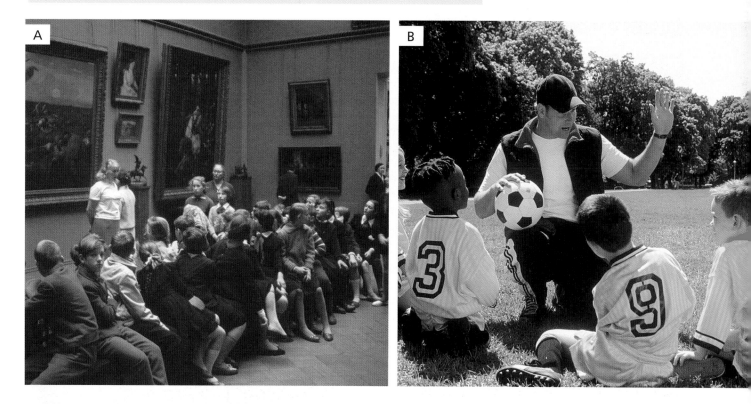

4   Compare and contrast the photographs. Use phrases and structures from Exercise 2 and vocabulary from Exercise 3 where possible.

1 Summarise the general content of the photographs, e.g. *Both pictures show …*

2 Say where you think the photos were taken and why, e.g. *Picture A looks like it's …*

3 Speculate about what is happening, e.g. *I think they might be …*

Reading 2

1 You are going to read descriptions of eight books. For questions 1–10, choose from the books A–G. As you read each question, highlight any important words or phrases. As you read about each book, look for 'parallel' words or phrases that link the book to a particular question. (The first one has been done for you.)

Which book would be good for someone who:

- is going to Sydney for a business conference who also wants to do some sightseeing during the weekend after the conference is over. (1) .... F

- used to love visiting friends in Australia but is now too old to travel so far. He would like something to show him what the country used to look like and what it looks like now. (2) ....

- is going to do a tour of Australia and wants to see as much as possible but doesn't have a lot of money. (3) ....

- has friends in Australia and New Zealand and never really understood the differences between the two countries. (4) ....

- wants to know why Australia seems to dominate world rugby and cricket. (5) ....

- has to write a school project about the early European settlers in Australia. (6) ....

- wants to buy a book as a present for a friend who is very interested in the Australian Aborigines. (7) ....

- loves reading about all kinds of animals. (8) ....

A Tamsin Berzins
A Guide To The Wildlife of Australia
Packed with information about Australian wildlife, this book is also full of stunning drawings. There is a special section on rare birds which is quite breathtaking!

B Marcus Bark-Jones
Australia: The Early Days
This is a collection of the writing of some of the first British arrivals in Australia. It describes the feelings and experiences of some remarkable people as they battled to make a life for themselves in this sometimes harsh new world.

C Kelly Richards
Budget Travel in Oz
A must-have guide for anybody travelling around Australia with an eye on their budget! Lots of suggestions for inexpensive food and accommodation and ways to get to see the best of Australia, but at bargain prices!

D Dr Graham Frinton
The Forgotten Discoverers
For anyone interested in the remarkable achievements and history of the Aborigines, this is the book to read. A detailed, objective account by a respected university scholar. Impressively researched and a fascinating read.

E Sheila Barton
So Near, Yet So Far
A hilarious look at the complex relationship between Australia and New Zealand. An eye-opener for many of us ignorant Europeans on what it's all about!

F Simon Horner
Australia in a Hurry!
This extensive guide to Australia is ideal for those who are short of time. With some excellent 'Day Plans', they show you how to spend full but varied days in each of the main Australian cities.

G Tilda Reckitt
Sporting Supremos
One of the greatest sporting nations in the world. A country where the people live and breathe sport of every kind and description. For all you sporting enthusiasts who want to know how the Australians got to be so good, here is the answer.

H Charlotte Hammond
A Visual Journey Down Under
This book is really a photographic journey through Australia over the last 40 years. With stunning pictures from all around the country, it both reminds one of the amazing variety that is Australia and also shows some of the ways the country is changing and developing.

2 Discuss with a partner which of these books you would most like to read. Say why.

Listening 2

1 How would you feel about living outside your country for a long time? What things would you miss? What things would you not be sorry to be away from?

2 Listen to a conversation in a coffee bar between Sally and her friend, Michael. Which of these things does Sally talk about?

> space   sport   being outside   nightlife
> beaches   friendliness   work   food

3 Listen again and decide if each statement below is true or false.

1 Sally thinks there is less space in Australian cities.
2 Sally says most Australians have houses with gardens.
3 Sally enjoys being outside.
4 Michael also likes being outside.
5 Sally likes going surfing.
6 Sally doesn't miss her friends now.
7 Sally thinks Europeans don't tend to be as friendly as Australians.
8 Sally loves the variety of food she can get in Australia.

Grammar 2: *so, neither, nor*

1 We can use *so* to mean *also* and *neither/nor* to mean *also not*. Look at these examples. In which of them do the people share the same situation or the same view?

A Australians love to be outside.   So do I.
B My parents went away for the weekend.   So did mine.
C I have never been surfing.   Neither/nor have I.
D I like lying on the beach.   I don't !

► Grammar reference 13.2 p. 145

2   Choose the correct alternatives below.

1 A Sophie hasn't finished her project.
   B Nor did Peter. / Nor has Peter.

2 A I can speak a little German.
   B So can I. / So have I.

3 A Her boyfriend is studying at the university.
   B So is mine. / So does mine.

4 A I love going horse-riding.
   B Nor do I. / I don't.

5 A We went to the beach on Saturday.
   B So did we. / Neither did we.

6 A We won't get a summer holiday this year.
   B Neither will we. / So do we.

3   Complete the responses below with one word in each case.

1 A I saw that new film with Penelope Cruz last night.
   B So .... I!

2 A I haven't done enough revision for tomorrow's test.
   B Nor .... I.

3 A I can't do my English homework.
   B Neither .... I.

4 A She's worked for this company for at least a year.
   B So .... I!

5 A We aren't going to the party tomorrow night.
   B Neither .... I.

6 A My sister always borrows my favourite clothes.
   B So .... mine!

7 A I won't see Paul until the weekend.
   B Nor .... I.

8 A I didn't use to play much sport when I was younger.
   B Neither .... I.

4   Write down five true sentences about yourself. Each sentence should use one of the following structures: present simple, present continuous, *can*, present perfect, past simple. Two of your sentences should be negative.

Example:

1 *I get up at the same time every day.*

2 *I'm playing football at the weekend.*

3 *I can't play a musical instrument.*

4 *I haven't been abroad.*

5 *I went shopping yesterday.*

5   Now work with other students. Take turns to say your sentences and respond as appropriate.

Example:

1 I get up at the same time every day. *(So do I. / I don't!)*

2 I'm playing football at the weekend. *(So am I. / I'm not!)*

3 I can't play a musical instrument. *(Neither/Nor can I. / I can!)*

4 I haven't been abroad. *(Neither/Nor have I. / I have!)*

5 I went shopping yesterday. *(So did I. / I didn't!)*

Writing: article

1   Read this task.

Task

You have just seen the following advertisement in a magazine. Read it carefully, then write an article for the magazine.

INTERNATIONAL TRAVEL WEEKLY

● *What is the most interesting place you have ever visited?*

● *What did you like about it?*

We are looking for short articles (120–140 words) answering these questions, and we will publish some of the best articles next month.

2   Before you write your article, look at the example opposite and answer these questions.

1   Does it keep to the subject of the task?

2   Does it have an interesting title?

3   Is it divided into appropriate paragraphs?

4   Are linking words used, e.g. *then, in addition*, etc.?

5   Is there a variety of interesting vocabulary?

6   Is the style formal or informal?

7   Is the spelling generally accurate?

8   Is it the right number of words?

9   Is the handwriting clear and easy to read?

3   Prepare to write your article. See Writing reference (Articles) on page 158. Follow these instructions.

1   Work with another student and choose a place together.

2   Brainstorm all the different things you both like about the place.

3   Decide how many paragraphs you are going to have and the subject of each one.

4   Decide on an interesting title.

The Magic Of Egypt

For the holiday of a lifetime, I definitely recommend a country which has incredible historical treasures, superb weather, dramatic scenery and an amazing variety of things to do and see. Of course, I am describing Egypt. I had wanted to visit Egypt ever since my best friend had a holiday there and showed me all her amazing photos. Obviously the first thing that everyone thinks of about Egypt is Cairo and the Pyramids. It certainly is fantastic to see them in the desert. But while you're in Cairo don't forget to go to the Khan El Khalili bazaar where you can buy souvenirs for all your family and friends. After Cairo, for luxury and relaxation, take a boat down the Nile to Luxor and Aswan. In Luxor, you can visit the ancient tombs in the Valley of the Kings and Queens, and you can see all the wonderful ancient Egyptian hieroglyphics at the temple of Karnak. Then, in Aswan, you can stay in one of the old colonial hotels and walk through the beautiful Kitchener's Island. As well as visiting all the historical sites, don't forget to try scuba diving in the Red Sea. The fish and coral are incredible. It's the perfect way to finish a holiday!

4   Write your article for the *International Travel Weekly* magazine (120–140 words). Check that you have answered both questions in the task in Exercise 1.

5   Show your article to another pair of students. Do they have any suggestions about how you might improve it? If necessary, rewrite your article.

► Unit writing test 13: Teacher's Book

UNIT 14 Elements of nature

Reading

1 Look at the pictures and discuss with a partner. How is each picture related to the sun?

Example: *In picture A, the people are on a beach. The woman is putting sun cream on her daughter.*

A

B

C

2 Quickly read the article about the sun. Find which paragraph refers to each picture.

Example: *Picture A: Paragraph 4 refers to people using sun cream.*

1 H

When there's sunshine, people are happy. Sunshine is popular and healthy. At least, in some ways it's healthy. It helps our bodies produce certain vitamins. It provides vitamin D which keeps our bodies healthy. The sun also stops us getting depressed.

2

When it's sunny, most people actually feel happier. They also behave in a more friendly way to others. If a country has a 'bad' summer when there's little sunshine, psychologists say you can clearly see that people become more miserable.

3

Until the 1930s, it was fashionable to have white skin. Then the fashion designer, Coco Chanel appeared in Paris with a suntan. It quickly became the fashionable thing to do and everyone wanted to have tanned skin.

4

Now we know more about the effects of sunshine than ever before. The negative aspects, for example skin cancer, are much more widely known. Many more people now use sun cream as protection from the sun.

5

Our weather systems are changing. The ten warmest years ever recorded were in the 1980s and 1990s. The oceans cover 72% of the Earth's surface and they take in huge amounts of heat from the sun.

6

As the Pacific Ocean becomes warmer it makes *El Niño* (a warm current of water along the west coast of South America) more powerful. This plays a part in creating disasters such as flooding as far away as Europe, India and northern China.

7

For centuries, people have been fascinated by the power of the sun. Some cultures have even based their religions on the sun. In Peru, they still celebrate the beginning of the Sun's New Year (the festival of *Inti Raymi*).

8

Perhaps we should consider more carefully what to do about the negative effects of the sun. Using more solar energy would be one way of using the sun's power in a positive way.

3   Read the list of headings below. Now read the article more carefully and choose the most suitable heading (A–H) for each part (1–8) of the article. Underline or highlight the parts of the article which helped you choose. (The first is done for you.)

A Dangers and diseases

B The first suntan

C Sun worship

D Mood changes

E A warmer world

F Using the power of the sun

G Global destruction

H Good for body and mind

4

1 The diagram below contains words from the article which are all connected to the word *sun*. Use the words to complete the sentences below.

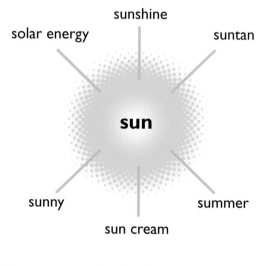

1 I love warm weather. My favourite season is
   ....

2 It's really important to put .... on your skin when the sun is strong.

3 A: What's the weather like where you are?
   B: It's quite ....

4 She came back from her holiday with a lovely
   ....

5 The park was full with people enjoying the
   ....

6 In our house, we use .... to heat the water.

2 Can you think of any other words connected to the word *sun*?

Grammar 1: nouns

1

1 Look at the picture and the example sentence and answer these questions.

1 Is it possible to count the word *weather* (e.g. *one weather, two weathers, three weathers,* etc.?)

2 Is it possible to count the word *problem* (e.g. *one problem, two problems, three problem,* etc.?)

The hot weather this summer has caused a lot of problems.

2 *Countable nouns* are things we can count and *uncountable nouns* are things we cannot count. Complete these sentences with the words in the box.

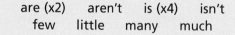

| are (x2)   aren't   is (x4)   isn't |
| few   little   many   much |

Countable nouns

Example: There ...*is*...... a bottle of sun cream in my bag.

1 There .... some dangers involved with sunbathing.

2 There .... any people on the beach.

3 .... there a shop near here?

4 .... there any shops near here?

5 There are a .... shops but not ....

Uncountable nouns

6 There .... some sun cream in my bag.

7 There .... any sun cream left.

8 .... there any sun cream left?

9 There is a .... sun cream left, but not
   ....

► Grammar reference 14.1 p. 145

2   Seven of the following sentences have mistakes in them. Find the mistakes and correct them.

1 Would you like a fruit?

2 Are there any water in the bucket?

3 I've moved some furniture around in the living room.

4 I'd like an information about the price of computers, please.

5 I haven't got any bread or milk.

6 There is some evidences of crime in the area.

7 She's got really bad headache.

8 Are there any people waiting to buy tickets?

9 I can't hear word you're saying.

10 I really need any advice about where to stay.

3

1 Some nouns have both countable and uncountable uses. Look at pictures A and B and match them with the correct sentences (1 and 2).

 1 Would you like *a chocolate*?

 2 Would you like *some chocolate*?

A

B

2 Look at the nouns in the box below. Which two **cannot** be used as both a countable and uncountable noun?

> chocolate   coffee   advice   chicken
> glass   hair   work   iron

▶ Grammar reference 14.1 p. 145

4   In each of these sentences, write *a* or *an* if necessary.

Examples: *She's got ....─........ hair down to her waist.*

 Would you like ..*a*........ glass of water?

1 I'll have .... chicken and chips, please.

2 I need .... new iron. Mine's broken.

3 Could you write .... coffee on the shopping list?

4 The new door is made entirely of .... glass.

5 Here, have .... chocolate. It's the last one.

6 I'd like .... cup of coffee with milk, please.

7 Oh no! There's .... hair in my soup.

8 The bridge is very strong because it's made of .... iron.

9 My uncle's got three pigs, two goats and .... old chicken.

10 You need sugar, ... chocolate and eggs for this recipe.

5

1 Complete each of these sentences with an appropriate countable or uncountable noun to make them true for you.

 1 For my next birthday, I'd like a
 ....

 2 I couldn't live without ....

 3 I eat .... every day.

 4 I never leave home without a
 ....

2 Compare your sentences with a partner. Explain your reasons for each sentence.

Vocabulary 1: the weather

1   Look at the phrases about the weather in the box. Divide them into four groups. Use a dictionary to help you if necessary.

> ~~it's sunny with a clear sky~~   it's really hot
> there's no wind   it's mild
> it's raining very hard   there's a pleasant breeze
> it's warm and pleasant   it's freezing   it's sunny
> it's cloudy   it's a dry day   it's very windy
> there's a thunderstorm   it's raining a little
> it's quite cold

hot/cold	sun/cloud	rain/no rain	wind/no wind
	it's sunny with a clear sky		

2   Work with a partner and answer these questions. Use the phrases in Exercise 1, making changes to the tenses where necessary.

1 What's the weather like today?

2 What's the weather usually like in your country in summer?

3 What's the weather usually like in your country in winter?

Listening 1: song

1   Look at the seven lines below (A–G) from a song. With a partner, decide if each line means the singer feels positive or negative.

A I felt the sun shining on my face.

B Like the stars above, I'm going to shine.

C I'm going to have a good time.

D I got rid of fears that were holding me.

E Everything is going my way.

F Everything is still going right.

G Not one thing can bring me down.

2

1 Read the words of the song. Think about where the missing lines (A–G) in Exercise 1 should go. Are there any that you are sure about?

2   Listen to the song and put the missing lines in Exercise 1 in the correct places.

Feelin' so good
Jennifer Lopez

When I opened up my eyes today – (1) ....
It became so clear to me that (2) ....
I feel like there's no limit to what I can see – (3) ....
My endless possibilities – has the whole world opened up for me?
That's why I'm feeling …
I'm feeling so good –
I knew I would.
Been taking care of myself – like I should. 'Cause (4) ....
Nothing in this world's going to turn me around.
Now the day is turning into night and (5) ....
There's no way you can stop me this time – or break this spirit of mine.
(6) .... – anything I want will be mine.
Tonight (7) .... – call a few friends of mine.
'Cause I'm loving life and tonight's for feeling…

3   The singer feels very positive about the sun shining on her face. How does the weather make you feel? Discuss these questions with other students, giving details and examples.

Example: *I feel really happy when it's hot and sunny. I always walk to school more quickly when it's sunny. I try to be outside all the time.*

1 How do you feel when the sun is shining and it's very hot? What do you do?

2 How do you feel when it's cloudy and raining? What do you do?

3 How do you feel when it's very windy and cold? What do you do?

4 How do you feel when it's raining very hard and there's a thunderstorm? What do you do?

121

Writing: transactional letter (2)

1

1 Read the letter that your friend Emilio has sent you. Why is Emilio writing to you?

> Dear ...
>
> **1** Thank you for your last letter. It sounds like you're having fun in London. I'm looking forward to coming to see you next weekend.
>
> **2** First of all, I'd like to go on the London Eye. I've heard that the views are fantastic, especially if the weather is good.
>
> **3** I hope it won't rain because I'd also like to visit some of London's famous parks. I've heard that Hyde Park is really beautiful.
>
> **4** If we can't be outside, could you find out what we could do inside? Perhaps we could go to a museum or something. See you on Friday evening.
>
> Best wishes
>
> Emilio

2 What does he write about in each paragraph?

Paragraph 1 *what he has learned from your last letter and what he's going to write about*

Paragraph 2 ....

....

Paragraph 3 ....

....

Paragraph 4 ....

....

2

1 Your writing will be easier to understand if you link the ideas in the paragraphs. Answer these questions about how to link ideas between paragraphs.

1 Which *linking phrase* helps link paragraph 1 to paragraph 2?
2 Look at the highlighted words in paragraphs 2 and 3. Emilio uses parallel words (words which refer to similar things) to link these paragraphs. Can you find the two parallel words that link paragraphs 3 and 4?

2 Look at the Writing reference (Paragraphs) on page 149. What is one other way of linking paragraphs?

3 Read the task below and answer these questions.

1 Who will you write to?
2 What information from the task will you include?
3 Will you include your own opinion?
4 How many words will you write?

Task

You are living and studying in London at the moment. A friend from your country is coming to visit you for two days next weekend. He/She has written you a letter asking for some information and your suggestions for the weekend. Write a letter to your friend. In your letter you should:

- give information about the weather
- give information about the London Eye, Hyde Park and the Science Museum
- give your opinion about what to do.

Write a letter of 120–140 words in an appropriate style. Do not write any addresses.

Weekend weather

London:
- Saturday a.m. – warm and sunny
- Saturday p.m. – getting a little cloudy
- Sunday a.m. – rain possible
- Sunday p.m. – cooler and more rain

Top ten sites in London

Hyde Park: A beautiful park in the heart of London. Have a picnic or hire a boat and go on the lake!

The London Eye: Flights last 30 minutes. No need to book – just come and enjoy the experience!

Science Museum: Seven floors of science. Not just for *looking at* – lots of interactive exhibits too!

4 Think about these questions.

1 What will you write in each paragraph?

2 How will you link the paragraphs together? (Look at the ideas in Exercise 2 to help you.)

5 Write your letter (120–140 words).

► Writing reference (Editing your writing) p. 153

6 Show your letter to a partner and read his/her letter. How has your partner linked the paragraphs?

Listening 2

1

1 What is an *eco-warrior*? With a partner, check that you understand the dictionary definition below.

between roads, environment by protesting.

eco-warrior /ˈiːkəʊ ˌwɒriə/ *n* [C] someone who tries to prevent damage to the environment by protesting against new roads, nuclear power, etc.

2 In the dictionary definition, it says that eco-warriors protest against new roads and nuclear power. What else do you think they usually protest about? Make a list with a partner.

2 Look at the photos and discuss the questions.

1 Picture A is of a typical eco-warrior in Britain. Do you have any similar kinds of people in your country?

2 Picture B is an eco-warrior called Rachel Carson. Do you think she is a typical eco-warrior? Why?/Why not?

3 What do you think the plane in picture C is doing?

3 Listen to a radio programme about Rachel Carson. Answer questions 2 and 3 in Exercise 2.

A

B

C

4 Read these sentences. Listen to the radio programme again and complete them.

1 Rachel Carson was probably the .... eco-warrior in the world.

2 She had a .... manner.

3 The name of her book was ....

4 In her book, she said that .... do a lot of damage to the environment.

5 Large companies and .... didn't want to listen to her.

6 DDT is a .... used in agriculture.

7 Some people who worked on the farms became ....

8 .... died because they ate food which had been sprayed.

5 Discuss these questions in small groups.

1 Think about your country and the whole world. What environmental problems have you heard about recently? Which do you think are the most important? Why?

2 What do you think about people who fight to protect the environment?

Grammar 2: articles

1 Look at these rules about using articles. Match each example (1–6) with the appropriate rule (a–f).

A
We use the indefinite article, *a/an* for:
a) single countable nouns mentioned for the first time
b) jobs.

B
We use the definite article, *the* for:
c) previously mentioned nouns
d) when there's only one of something.

C
We use no article for:
e) most streets, towns, cities, countries and names
f) uncountable, plural and abstract nouns.

1 She wrote a *book*.
2 The *book* was a best seller.
3 She was born in *Britain*.
4 She was a *scientist*.
5 Humans are destroying *nature*.
6 The *Earth* is being destroyed.

▶ Grammar reference 14.2 p. 145

2 Complete this text by writing *a*, *an*, *the* or *X* (if there is no article necessary).

Water is essential for (1) ....X...... life. People can live for weeks without (2) .... food. But they can only live for a few days without water. The driest place on Earth is in the Atacama Desert in (3) .... Chile. This area receives about 0.1 mm of rain per year. Because it is so dry, it is similar to (4) .... moon and some parts have been used for scientific experiments. People in other areas have invented ways of 'creating' (5) .... water. In one village, Chungungo, they have created (6) .... system of nets. This allows them to collect water from (7) .... fog. (8) .... system consists of (9) .... large net laid on the side of a mountain. As fog passes over (10) .... net, water condenses and runs through pipes into (11) .... collection area.

3 Look back at the letter you wrote in the previous *Writing* section (or another piece of writing that you've done recently).

1 Underline examples of the different uses of articles listed in Exercise 1 (*definite article, indefinite article* and *no article*).

2 Have you used them correctly? Check with a partner.

Vocabulary 2: phrasal verbs

1

1 Look at these sentences. Match the phrasal verbs in italics with the definitions in the box.

1 She *took on* governments and companies in her fight to save the environment.
2 People *took to* her quiet manner immediately.
3 It was hard for people to *take in* the importance of her ideas.

to understand completely
to like (somebody) when you first meet
to challenge

2 Now match the phrasal verbs in italics in the sentences below with the definitions in the box.

to have a holiday from work
to start (a new hobby)
to admit that you were wrong
to look or behave like an older relative
to get control and responsibility (for something)

1 I want to get fit so I've decided to *take up* jogging.
2 I'm sorry that I upset you. I *take back* everything I said.
3 Tina *takes after* her mother. She's got the same eyes and the same temper.
4 Who do you think will *take over* the department when Johnny leaves?
5 You look ill. Why not *take* a few days *off*?

▶ Grammar reference 5.2 p. 140

2 Complete these sentences with the correct word from the box.

| after | back | in | off |
| on | over | to | up |

1 She was very rude to me yesterday. But today she took it all ....

2 I'm feeling really ill. I think I'm going to take the rest of the day ....

3 Ricky has got very fit since he took .... rollerblading last year.

4 When he told me about the accident, it was difficult to take it ....

5 We took .... a team from a school nearby – and we won the match!

6 She takes .... her mother in appearance but not personality.

7 Julia is really lovely. When I first met her, I took .... her immediately.

8 I'd like to take .... my dad's business when I'm older.

3 Ask and answer these questions with a partner.

1 Who do you take after in your family? In what ways?

2 When was the last time you took time off school/work? What for?

3 Can you describe a time when you wanted to take back what you'd said to someone?

4 What was the last hobby you took up? Do you still do it? Why?/Why not?

Speaking

1

1 What is the connection between these pictures?

2 Read these questions and listen to two students, Pablo and Erica, talking about the pictures. Do they answer question 1, question 2 or both?

1 Which of these things do you have in your town, your house, your school or your work?

2 Which three are the biggest problems where you live?

2

1 Listen again. Which of these phrases do Pablo and Erica use?

Giving an opinion: *I think …   In my opinion …*
Agreeing: *That's right.   I agree up to a point, but …*
Disagreeing: *Oh, I don't really agree.   I don't agree at all!*

2 Work with a partner. Look again at the pictures and discuss the questions in Exercise 1.2. You can use some of the phrases above.

3

1 Listen to another part of Pablo and Erica's discussion. Which of these questions are they discussing?

1 Is it important to buy recycled paper?
2 What would you do to improve your town?
3 Should people pay to use their cars in cities?
4 How important is it to stop people dropping litter on the streets?

2 Listen again. Which of these phrases do they use?

Pausing to think: *Well, it depends …   I'm not sure, but …*
Asking for an opinion: *What do you think?   What about you?   Do you agree?*

3 Complete the dialogue by choosing the correct word from the box.

about	agree	depends
	sure	think

A: I think some more trees would really improve this town. Do you (1) ....?

B: Well, it (2) .... We need more seating areas, too. What do you (3) ....?

A: Yes, it would be nice to have more seats and benches. I also think that more litter bins would be a big improvement. What (4) .... you?

B: I'm not (5) ...., but you're probably right.

4 Work with a partner and discuss the questions in Exercise 3.1.

▶ Unit test 14: Teacher's Book

The business of food

Reading

1 Answer these questions. Then compare your answers with a partner.

1 How often do you buy chewing gum?
  A every day
  B sometimes
  C never

2 Why do you (or most people) use chewing gum?
  A to help relax
  B to stop smoking
  C to prevent tooth decay

3 What do you think is the worst thing about chewing gum?
  A people look silly chewing
  B it makes a lot of litter and mess
  C it's a waste of money

4 Which brands of chewing gum are popular in your country?

2 Discuss these questions with a partner.

1 Do you know anything about the process of making chewing gum?

2 Is chewing gum mostly made of natural or man-made materials?

3 Now read the article and check your answers to the questions in Exercise 2.

4

1 Read the list of headings below. Then look at the example. Which parts of the article tell you that heading H goes with paragraph 1?

  A The beginning of chewing gum
  B Taking gum to the factories
  C Extracting gum from the trees
  D Using non-natural products
  E The discovery of different gum trees
  F How chewing gum can help you
  G Many people buy chewing gum
  H Many chewing gum producers

2 Now read the article more carefully and choose the most suitable heading (A–H) for each part (1–8). Highlight or underline the words and expressions which helped you choose.

Sticky Business

1 | H |
Thousands of different brands of chewing gum are available in the shops today. They have different logos, but the products inside are very similar. Each company tries to find different ways of selling their product.

2
Some producers say that chewing gum helps you both concentrate and relax. Recent TV advertisements also tell us that 20 minutes of chewing can prevent tooth decay. Research has shown that when people are told this, sales increase.

3
It's big business now, but chewing gum is not a modern invention. For centuries, the ancient Greeks chewed gum. The gum was obtained from mastic trees, which were found mainly in Greece and Turkey.

4
It was in the 19th century, however, that the process of making modern chewing gum was developed. In the late 1860s, chicle was discovered in sapodilla trees in the Mexican rainforest. Gum made from chicle is much smoother and more elastic than gum from mastic trees.

Grammar 1: passives

1 Discuss these questions with a partner.

1 The verbs in the sentences below are *passive* forms. Do they describe:
a) the *people* involved in making chewing gum?
b) the *process* involved in making chewing gum?
*Chewing gum **is made** from man-made products.*
*Chewing gum **was made** from natural products before.*

2 Look at these examples. When we don't know or we are not interested in *who* did something (the agent), do we usually use the *active* form or the *passive* form of the verb?
*Someone **built** this house in 1960.*
*This house **was built** in 1960.*

3 Look at these examples. Which sentence is more likely? Why?
This house was built in 1960 by someone.
This house was built in 1960 by my grandfather.

2 Look back at the article about chewing gum and highlight or underline other examples of the present simple passive and the past simple passive.

▶ Grammar reference 15.1 p. 146

3 Read the first sentence in each pair and say what tense the underlined verb is.

Example: The largest collection of chewing gum brands is owned by Johanna Bauenmand in Copenhagen. *present simple passive*

1 £120 million is spent on chewing gum in the UK every year.
People in the UK ....

2 The biggest gum bubble was blown in California.
Someone in California ....

3 Sugar-free gum is used to keep teeth healthy.
People ....

4 People in the UK consume 900 million litres of bottled water every year.
900 million litres of bottled water ....

5 Last year, the UK imported 25% of its bottles of water from Asia.
Last year, 25% of the UK's bottles of water ....
....

6 Farmers grow square watermelons inside glass boxes.
Square watermelons ....

5
The process of collecting chicle from the rainforests is difficult. Chicle flows more easily before the sun comes up, so it is usually collected at night. The chicle collectors (*chicleros*) go into the hot, humid forests and climb up the sapodilla trees in the dark.

6
When it comes out of the tree, chicle is liquid and therefore difficult to transport. So it is heated on small fires. When it cools down, it is made into large sticky blocks. These are then transported to production centres. The price paid for a kilo of gum when it leaves the forest is $1.75. When it reaches the shops, consumers pay about 100 times that price.

7
It is getting more difficult for the *chicleros* to make a living, however. Many alternatives to chicle have been developed and the main part of chewing gum is now man-made. Only a few natural products are used to help improve the flavour and the texture. As a result, the *chicleros* find it difficult to sell their product to the big companies.

8
The companies have no difficulty in selling to the consumer, however. Chewing gum is big business. If all the pieces of chewing gum produced every year were laid end to end, they would stretch to the moon and back six times!

4 For each question in Exercise 3, finish the second sentence so that it means the same as the first, starting with words given.

Example: The largest collection of chewing gum brands <u>is owned</u> by Johanna Bauenmand in Copenhagen.

Johanna Bauenmand in Copenhagen owns the largest collection of chewing gum brands.

5

1 Work in pairs and think of a film that you both know. Don't tell other pairs which one you have chosen. Write a short description of the film, using these questions and any other information you know. Use the passive where necessary.

When was it made?
Where was it filmed?
Who was it written by?
Who was it directed by?
Who are the main characters played by?
Where/When is it set?

2 Now work in small groups. Read your description to the other students, but don't say the name of the film. Can you guess which films other students are describing?

Vocabulary 1: buying goods

1 Look at the words in italics in questions 1–8. Write the correct word next to each dictionary definition (A–H).

1 What is your favourite *brand* of sports clothes?

2 Can you describe the *logo* of that brand?

3 Can you remember a good *advertisement* you've seen recently on TV?

4 What *product* is it advertising?

5 Which *company* produces it?

6 Which *market* do you think it is for?

7 Which do you think *consumers* prefer: cheap goods with little packaging, or more expensive goods with more attractive packaging? Why?

8 *Research* shows that people don't like eating blue food. Why do you think this is?

A Something that is made or grown to be sold:
  product

B An organisation that makes or sells goods or services:
  ....

C The official sign of a company: ....
D A general word for people who buy things: ....
E The group of people who buy a particular product:
  ....

F A short film on TV to persuade people to buy something:
  ....

G A detailed study to find out new information: ....

H Something produced by a company with its own particular name and style: ....

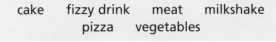 **2** Check that you can pronounce the words in Exercise 1 correctly, using a dictionary if necessary. Then listen to the questions on the recording and check your pronunciation.

3 Work in small groups. Ask and answer the questions in Exercise 1.

Listening

1 Look at the words in the box and match them with the correct pictures (A–F).

cake   fizzy drink   meat   milkshake
pizza   vegetables

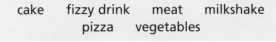 **2** Listen to six short extracts and number the things in Exercise 1 in the order you hear them.

Example: *pizza – 1*

3

1 Look at these questions. Is each question asking about:

- content (what the people are talking about)?
- relationship (what the relationship between the people is)?
- attitude (what the attitude of the speaker is)?

1 What kind of pizza does she order? *content*

2 What are the students learning about? ....

3 What is the woman's connection to the people? ....

4 What is special about takeaway lunches? ....

5 How does the man feel about the preparations? ....

6 What does he want you to do? ....

2 Read the possible answers below. Listen to the extracts again and answer the questions.

1 A woman is making a phone call. What kind of pizza does she order?
   A a large pizza with ham only
   B an extra large pizza with ham only
   C an extra large pizza with ham and pineapple

2 A man is talking to a class of students. What are the students learning about?
   A how to repair machines
   B how to cook
   C how to design kitchens

3 A woman is talking to a group of people. What is the woman's connection to the people?
   A She's their mother.
   B She's their teacher.
   C She's their doctor.

4 You hear an announcer in a shop. What is special about takeaway lunches?
   A You get one free fizzy drink.
   B You get two free fizzy drinks.
   C You get two fizzy drinks but only pay for one.

5 Two people are talking about party preparations. How does the man feel about the preparations?
   A worried
   B annoyed
   C relaxed

6 A man speaks to you in the street. What does he want you to do?
   A buy something
   B comment on something
   C give him something

Grammar 2: causative *have*

1

1 Look at the pictures. What does the woman say in each one?

I'm going to make the cake.

I'm going to have the cake made.

A

B

2 Answer these questions with a partner.

1 In which picture is she going to make the cake herself?

2 In which picture is she going to ask someone else to make the cake for her?

3 When we say that we are going to ask someone to do something, we use *have* + something (e.g. *a cake*) + ...

▶ Grammar reference 15.2 p. 146

2

1 What other services can you ask someone to do for you?

Example: *You can have pizzas delivered.*

2 Complete these sentences with the correct form of the verb *have* and the past participle.

Example: I ...*had*.... three pizzas ...*delivered*... (*deliver*) yesterday.

1 I've decided to .... the food .... (*prepare*) in advance.

2 Carolina .... her hair .... (*cut*) yesterday.

3 I .... the car .... (*wash*) already.

4 We need to .... the roof .... (*repair*) very soon.

5 I .... my passport photograph .... (*take*) at 10.00 tomorrow.

6 Judith .... her jacket .... (*clean*) last week.

7 Where can I .... my watch .... (*mend*)?

8 We .... the house .... (*paint*) at the moment.

3 Ask and answer these questions with a partner. Talk about yourself or someone in your family. Give details and reasons.

Example: *I usually have my hair cut. I cut it myself once and it looked terrible. I usually go every eight weeks …*
My dad usually repairs the car himself. He doesn't like having it done somewhere else. He says it's too expensive …

Do you (or does someone in your family) usually …

1 cut your hair or have it cut?

2 repair broken machines or have them repaired?

3 go and buy your own food or have it delivered?

4 clean your own things (car, bedroom, shoes, etc.) or have them cleaned?

Use of English: transformations

1 Look at these pairs of sentences. For each pair decide if the two sentences have similar or different meanings.

Example:
a) Someone else is cutting my hair tomorrow.
b) I'm having my hair cut tomorrow.
similar meanings

1 a) I cleaned my shoes yesterday.
b) I had my shoes cleaned yesterday.

2 a) Brazil exports a lot of very good coffee.
b) A lot of very good coffee is exported from Brazil.

3 a) Paula can run faster than Sharon.
b) Sharon can run as fast as Paula.

4 a) The meal was more expensive than I expected.
b) I expected the meal to be cheaper.

5 a) They weren't old enough to see the film.
b) They were too young to see the film.

6 a) They will take the rubbish away tomorrow.
b) The rubbish will be taken away tomorrow.

7 a) 'Have you been a firefighter for long?' he asked her.
b) He asked her if she had been a firefighter for long.

8 a) You are not allowed to eat in this area.
b) You don't have to eat in this area.

9 a) If it rains, we will go home.
b) We won't go home unless it rains.

10 a) She's my best friend although I haven't known her for very long.
b) I haven't known her for very long but she's my best friend.

11 a) You'd better go to the dentist.
b) If I were you, I'd go to the dentist.

12 a) Most of the students left early.
b) Hardly any of the students left early.

2 Now complete the second sentence in each pair below so that it means the same as the first. Write between one and three words. Refer to the examples in Exercise 1 for help where necessary.

Example:
a) Someone else is cutting my hair tomorrow.
b) I'm ...*having my hair*... cut tomorrow.

1 a) I'm going to ask someone to repair my computer.
b) I'm going .... my computer repaired.

2 a) Somebody cleaned my car
yesterday.
  b) My car ....
yesterday.

3 a) The book was more interesting
than the film.
  b) The film wasn't ....
.... the book.

4 a) This maths equation is more
complicated than the last one.
  b) The last maths equation was
.... this one.

5 a) She was too far away for him to
hear her.
  b) He wasn't ....
.... to hear her.

6 a) He is giving the presentation this
afternoon.
  b) The presentation ....
.... this afternoon.

7 a) 'Are you going to the party
tonight?' she asked him.
  b) She asked him ....
.... going to the party
that night.

8 a) Simon mustn't eat any salt.
  b) Simon isn't ....
.... eat any salt.

9 a) Unless you start working, you will
fail the exam.
  b) If ....
working, you will fail the exam.

10 a) They tried to help but couldn't do
anything useful.
  b) Although ....
help, they couldn't do anything
useful.

11 a) If I were you, I'd change your job.
  b) You'd ....
change your job.

12 a) She was known by most of the
teachers.
  b) Nearly ....
knew her.

Vocabulary 2: food

1

1 **Look at the man in the picture. His name is John Machin and he has a very unusual type of diet. Discuss how you think John would answer these questions.**

  1 Do you feel healthy?
  2 What do you eat?
  3 Do you like what you eat?

2 **Now read his answers and see if you were correct.**

1

*I've never liked meat and when I was a
teenager, I became a **vegetarian**. I also stopped drinking
milk. It made me ill because it was too **fatty** for my stomach
to digest. In my twenties, I decided to eat even more simply.
Now I feel healthier than ever before.*

2

*I don't need a **cooker** in my house any more
because I only eat **raw** food. Every meal I have is a 'mono'
meal – I only eat one thing during a meal. In fact, I now restrict
my diet to only brazil nuts, coconuts and oranges,
and I never combine these in one meal.*

3

*People often ask me if I get bored. The answer is
not at all. Everything I eat tastes delicious. When you cook
food, most of the goodness goes out of it. My food gives me
both **savoury** and **sweet** flavours and all the goodness
my body needs.*

2

1 Look at the pairs of words below. Some of them are from what John says in Exercise 1. For each pair of words, what is the difference in meaning?

Example: *a cook = a person who prepares and cooks food*
a cooker = a large machine in the kitchen used for cooking

1 a cook/a cooker (nouns)
2 a vegetable/a vegetarian (nouns)
3 rare/raw (adjectives)
4 savoury/sweet (adjectives)
5 fatty/fattening (adjectives)
6 to boil/to fry (verbs)
7 to bake/to roast (verbs)

2 Check the pronunciation of the words in a dictionary if necessary.

3   Complete these sentences with the words in Exercise 2.

Example: Peas are the only <u>vegetables</u> that Daniel likes.

1 Oh, don't cook the carrots. I prefer them ....

2 I used to be a ...., but now I eat chicken.

3 It's not very good for you to eat a lot of .... foods like chips.

4 Would you like your steak ...., medium or well-done?

5 Can you get me some water? I want to .... the potatoes.

6 Can you turn the .... on, please? I'm going to .... this chicken for lunch.

7 I've decided I'm going to .... a cake for Kate's birthday.

8 I need some oil to .... these chips.

9 Susanna is trying to lose weight. She doesn't eat any .... food.

10 My mum prefers .... things (like biscuits) but my dad prefers .... things (like crisps).

11 I love cooking and I'd like to get a job as a ....

Speaking

1

1 Look at these pictures. With a partner, check you know what each item is.

2 You're going to do a speaking task. Before you start speaking, check the language for making suggestions (on page 76) and coming to a decision (on page 85).

2   You're planning to have a picnic with a group of friends. You are going to a large park and the weather is hot and sunny. Look again at the pictures in Exercise 1. With a partner, say which of the things people usually take on picnics. Then decide on three of the items you would most like to take on your picnic. You can use the language you found in Exercise 1.2.

3

1 Look at the phrases below for pausing to think about your opinion, giving your opinion, asking someone for his/her opinion, agreeing and disagreeing. Rewrite them in the correct order.

Example: really I agree don't – *I don't really agree.*

1 agree all don't I at
2 right I you're think
3 depends many Well, on it things
4 opinion, eat much my people too In
5 sure, I'm right but not probably you're
6 point, fattening agree drinks to a but up fizzy I are

2 Listen and check your answers. Repeat the sentences with the correct pronunciation.

4

1 Read these questions. For each one, think about your opinion and your reasons.

1 Do you eat healthy food for breakfast?
2 How popular are fast foods in your country?
3 You should eat five pieces of fruit every day. Do you think this is good advice?
4 Which food would you miss most if you couldn't have it?

2 Now discuss the questions with your partner. Use some of the phrases in Exercise 3.

Writing: report (2)

1 Read this task. How many things will you write about in your report?

Task

When young people come to Britain to learn English, they usually stay with British families. These families need to know what kind of food young people from your country like eating.

You have been asked by the British Tourist Centre to write a report describing the eating preferences of young people in your country, including what they usually like, what they usually don't like and typical meal times.

2 Which of the following sentences use formal language and which informal language?

1 I'm going to write about what young people like eating.
2 This report will consider the eating preferences of young people.

▶ Writing reference (Formal and informal language) p. 151

3

1 Reports are usually written using formal language. Which of the following phrases could you include in a report? Which should you not include?

Introduction
1 The aim of this report is to describe …
2 This report considers …
3 I've had some really interesting conversations with students in my school and …

Eating preferences
4 Firstly, most young people's eating preferences include …
5 My friend Sarah really likes pasta …
6 Generally, at the start of the day, young people in my country prefer …

Conclusion
7 Therefore, I would recommend that …
8 To conclude, most young people …
9 So, anyway, I think that it's a good idea if …

2 Look at the Writing reference (Reports) on page 157. What other useful formal language can you find?

4 You are going to do the task in Exercise 1. First discuss these questions.

1 How many paragraphs do you need to write?
2 Can you use headings for the paragraphs?
3 What three points do you need to include in the second paragraph?

▶ Writing reference (Reports) p. 157

5 Write your report using about 120–140 words. Use the paragraph plan and the appropriate phrases in Exercise 3 to help you.

▶ Progress test 5: Teacher's Book

1 Rewrite these sentences with *like* in the correct order.

1 like cinema you to the would go to?

2 like mine some got just Maria's jeans

3 like homework my doing her doesn't sister

4 like teacher my one isn't my last new

5 like I have dinner she would some Aya asked to if

6 like Yuri magazines about reading Costas computers and

7 like think brother I look my do you?

8 like year to Majorca to on go holiday I'd next

9 like that book film is I very the think the

10 like buses I for or waiting don't trains

2 Rewrite these sentences, replacing the underlined part of the sentence with the correct form of one of the phrasal verbs in the box. You may need to make small changes to other parts of the sentence.

take to   take on   take in   take up
take after   take back
take (time) off   take over

1 You're too busy to <u>accept</u> any more work.

2 You should try to get fit. Why don't you <u>start</u> jogging?

3 She was ill last week. She <u>had three days 'holiday' from work</u>.

4 I found it difficult to <u>understand completely</u> the bad news.

5 She <u>got responsibility for</u> the project when her boss left the company.

6 I can't believe how much you <u>look and behave like</u> your father.

7 That was horrible! I hope you will <u>admit what you said was wrong</u>.

8 My brother is a very friendly person. Everyone <u>likes him when they first meet him</u> immediately.

3 Match each sentence with the correct response in the box.

So do I.   So will I.   Nor am I.   So have I.
Nor will I.   So can I.   Nor did I.
Nor do I.   So did I.   Nor can I.
So am I.   Nor have I.

1 I can speak two languages. ....

2 I won't phone him. ....

3 I like chocolate. ....

4 I didn't go to the meeting. ....

5 I haven't seen John today. ....

6 I'm taking an exam next week. ....

7 I can't swim very well. ....

8 I'll see Billy tomorrow. ....

9 I've been to Canada. ....

10 I watched a film last night. ....

11 I'm not catching the next train. ....

12 I don't live in a big city. ....

4 Complete these sentences using one of the words from the box. Sometimes the word needs to be plural. Use *a* or *an* if necessary.

blood   evidence   headache   information
meat   minute   person   photograph
queue   space   sugar   supermarket

1 Do you take .... in your coffee?

2 Wait ....! I'm just coming.

3 Vegetarians don't eat ....

4 We need to get .... about where to stay.

5 I cut my finger and there was .... all over my shirt.

6 Can you tell me if there's .... near here?

7 How many .... came to the party?

8 We're moving to a bigger house because we need more ....

9 Don't forget your camera. You'll want to take lots of ....

10 When I got to the bus stop, there was .... of people waiting.

11 There wasn't much .... at the scene of the crime.

12 Have you got any aspirin? I've got ....

5 Unjumble the letters to make words about the physical world and tourism.

1 The last .... *tocuryn* I went to on holiday was France.

2 Is it a long .... *gflith* from London to Moscow?

3 I'll meet you at the .... *prartio* – Terminal 2.

4 The *Titanic* sank in the Atlantic .... *acone*.

5 Asia is the biggest .... *nectotinn* in the world.

6 I bought some perfume and some CDs in .... *tydu-refe*.

7 I bought lots of .... *senorvusi* in London, including three T-shirts.

8 We took a small boat over to a beautiful .... *lidans* for the day.

9 You need to wear strong boots for climbing in the .... *staminnou*.

10 Let's do some .... *thensiseigg*. I'd like to see the Houses of Parliament.

11 Be careful when you go to the .... *seerdt*. It's very hot and dry.

12 This .... *bodukiego* tells you everything you need to know about Amsterdam.

6 Complete the second sentence in each pair so that it means the same as the first. Write between one and three words.

1 They export a lot of cars from Japan.
A lot of cars .... from Japan.

2 In most hotels, your room is cleaned every day.
In most hotels, ... your room every day.

3 The hairdresser cut my hair really short last time.
I had .... really short last time.

4 Where can someone repair my car?
Where .... my car repaired?

5 Last year, they transported all their goods by road.
Last year, all their goods .... by road.

6 Three men are painting our house at the moment.
We .... our house painted by three men at the moment.

7 When did someone invent the telephone?
When .... invented?

8 The shop is going to develop my holiday photos tomorrow.
I'm going .... my holiday photos developed tomorrow.

9 They invited over 150 people to the party.
Over 150 people .... to the party.

10 The cleaner's on the corner always cleans my jacket.
I always .... cleaned at the cleaner's on the corner.

7 Choose the correct alternative – A, B, C or D – to complete each of these sentences about buying and selling, and food and cooking.

1 I love eating cakes, biscuits, chocolate and other .... things.
A savoury B sweet C raw D rare

2 Be careful of the hot water. I'm going to .... the carrots.
A fry B bake C boil D roast

3 She's decided not to eat meat and become a ....
A cook B cooker C vegetable D vegetarian

4 The .... of my favourite T-shirt company is a small blue star.
A logo B brand C product D market

5 Food which contains a lot of sugar is very ....
A rare B raw C fatty D fattening

6 They've done a lot of .... into what people like eating.
A advertisement B research C market D product

7 I don't buy just one .... of trainers – it depends what's cheapest.
A market B brand C logo D product

8 Jack likes eating .... food, like salad, which doesn't need cooking.
A raw B rare C savoury D sweet

Grammar reference

UNIT 1

1.1 Question words and direct questions

There are three main types of questions:

1 *Yes/No* questions (the expected answer is *yes* or *no*)

   A *Are you Spanish?*
   B *Yes, I am.*

2 *Wh-* questions (*Who? Whose? Where? Why? What? Which? When?* and also *How?*)

   What did you say?
   Whose bag is that?
   When does the film start?

3 Alternative questions (the expected answer is one of two options)

   *Do you want to phone him **now** or **later**?*
   *Which do you prefer, **the theatre** or **the cinema**?*

1.1A *Yes/No* questions

Form

With *be, have (got)* and modal verbs like *may, can, could would* and *should*, we form the question by changing the order of the subject and the verb.

He's got a new computer. = ***Has he got** a new computer?*

***Are you going** out now?*
***Should I go** to the dentist?*
***Did he see** you?*

With other verbs we use *Do/Does/Did* + subject + infinitive.

***Do you like** coffee?*
***Does he live** in Greece?*
***Did they go** to the party?*

1.1B *Wh-* questions

a) Form

Wh- question word + auxiliary + subject + main verb

Where are they going?

What did you do?
Why was she here?

b) Questions about the subject

We don't use the auxiliary and we don't change the order of the subject and verb. The word order is the same as it is for statements.

Contrast:

***Who saw** that film last night?* (question about the subject)
***What makes** you frightened?* (question about the subject)

With:

***Who did he go** to the party with?* (question about the object)
***What do you have** for breakfast?* (question about the object)

1.1C Alternative questions

There are two types of alternative questions. In one type the word order is like a *Yes/No* question and in the other the word order is like a *Wh-* question.

***Would you like** pasta or pizza?*
***Where shall we go** on holiday, to Spain or Greece?*

1.2 Indirect questions

a) Use

Indirect questions are more polite than direct questions.

Direct: *How old are you?* (neutral)
Indirect: *Could you tell me how old you are?* (more polite)

b) Form

- For all indirect questions, we don't use the auxiliary and we don't change the order of the subject and verb. The word order is the same as it is for statements.
- For indirect *Yes/No* questions, we use *if* or *whether*.

whether ≠ (climate) weather

- Two common ways of starting indirect questions are:

  Could you tell me (if/whether) …
  I'd like to know (if/whether) …
  Could you tell me how old you are? (*How old are you?*)
  I'd like to know where you are from. (*Where are you from?*)
  Could you tell me if/whether you like swimming? (*Do you like swimming?*)
  I'd like to know if/whether you arrived on time this morning? (*Did you arrive on time this morning?*)

UNIT 2

2.1 Present continuous

a) Form

The present form of *be* + the *-ing* form of the verb
Contracted forms: *I'm (I am), you're (you are), s/he's (s/he is), it's (it is), we're (we are), they're (they are), + -ing* form

b) Use

We use the present continuous when we are talking about:

1 actions happening now

PAST   NOW   FUTURE

Jim's reading in the living room.

2 temporary situations

PAST   NOW   FUTURE

I'm working in a restaurant for the summer.

3 plans and arrangements in the future.

PAST   NOW   10:00 tomorrow morning   FUTURE

They're meeting at 10 o'clock tomorrow morning.

2.2 Present simple

a) Form

- Positive statements
  I/you/we/they **live** in New York.

- Negative statements
  I/you/we/they **don't live** in New York.
  He/she/it **doesn't live** in New York.
- Questions
  Do *I/you/we/they* **live** in New York?
  Does *he/she/it* **live** in New York?
- Short answers
  Yes, *I/you/we/they* **do**.
  No, *I/you/we/they* **don't**.
  Yes, *he/she/it* **does**.
  No, *he/she/it* **doesn't**.

b) Use

We use the present simple:

1 with routine or regular repeated actions (often with adverbs of frequency, e.g. *always, sometimes* – see 2.3)

  I **play** football **every Sunday afternoon**.
  He **doesn't eat** meat.
  They **sometimes work** late on Friday.

2 when we are talking about permanent situations

  He **lives** in a small town by the sea.
  Do you come from Brazil?

3 with state verbs which are not normally used in continuous forms: *be, have, depend, know, think, understand, disagree, like, want, hear, love, see, smell, taste*

  I **am** very thirsty – *I* **want** a drink.
  I **don't understand**.

4 in spoken instructions, systems and processes.

  You **go** straight on and **take** the first turning on the left.
  First, you **turn** it on, then you **put** the disk in.

2.3 Adverbs of frequency

a) Use

Adverbs of frequency say *how often* something happens. We can use one word or a phrase.

Examples:
always, usually, often, sometimes, occasionally, never, every Sunday, once a week, every morning

b) Form

1 Generally, adverbs of frequency come:

- after auxiliary verbs
  I **don't usually** have breakfast.
  She's **never** been skiing before.
- after the verb *to be*
  He **is always** so kind!
  We **are often** away at the weekend.

- before other verbs.
  *She **sometimes arrives** late.*
  *I **occasionally get** emails from Francesca.*

2 Other positions of adverbs of frequency in a sentence:

- *Usually, often, sometimes* and *occasionally* can come at the beginning or at the end of a clause.
  ***Usually** my brother gets up first in my family.*
  *I walk to school **sometimes**.*

- *Always* and *never* don't come at the beginning or at the end of a clause.
  ~~*Always I play football on Sundays.*~~
  ~~*He phones me never.*~~

- Longer phrases must come at the beginning or at the end of a clause.
  *I visit my grandmother **once a week**.*
  ***On Sunday mornings** I get up really late.*

UNIT 3

3.1 Gerunds

A gerund is the *-ing* form of a verb when it is used like a noun.

a) Gerunds after prepositions
We use gerunds when the verb is immediately after a preposition.

*I'm looking forward **to hearing** from you.*
*She's afraid **of speaking** in public.*

b) Gerunds as *subjects*
We use gerunds when we are talking about an action or activity in a general way.

***Using** a computer a lot is bad for your eyes.*
***Lying** on the beach is really relaxing.*

3.2 Gerunds and infinitives

3.2A Verbs followed by the gerund form *-ing*

*The project **involved using** the Internet.*

Here are some common verbs which are followed by the gerund:

avoid, can't stand, consider, dislike, enjoy, finish, give up, imagine, involve, mind, practise, suggest, understand

3.2B Verbs followed by an infinitive with *to*

*She **managed to swim** 25 metres under water.*

Here are some common verbs which are followed by an infinitive with *to*:

afford, agree, appear, arrange, ask, choose, decide, expect, hesitate, hope, learn, manage, offer, plan, promise, refuse, want

UNIT 4

4.1 Past simple

a) Form
Verb + *-ed* (remember there are many irregular verb forms)

b) Use
We use the past simple:

1 to talk about events in the past which are now finished
  *I **went** to an Italian restaurant last night.*
  *He **walked** into the shop, **found** a magazine and **paid** for it.*

2 to talk about situations in the past
  *When she **was** a child, she lived in Paris.*

3 in reported speech (for more on this, see 5.1).
  *He **said he didn't like** parties.*

4.2 Past continuous

a) Form
was/were + *-ing*

b) Use
We use the past continuous:

1 to talk about actions in progress in the past
  *I **was watching** a really good film on TV.*

2 to talk about an event that was in progress when another event happened

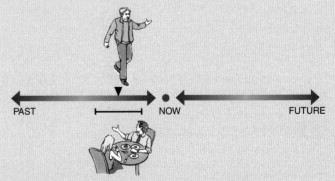

*They **were having** lunch when Daniel arrived.*

3 to talk about actions in progress at the same time in the past.
*While I **was tidying** my room, my brother **was playing** computer games.*

4.3 Past perfect simple

a) Form

had + past participle

b) Use

We use the past perfect simple:

1 to talk about a time earlier than another past time

9.30	10.00

*When we arrived, the concert **had finished**.*

2 in reported speech (for more on this, see 5.1).
*She said she **had booked** the tickets.*

UNIT 5

5.1 Direct speech and reported speech

5.1A Direct speech

This is when we report the exact words that someone says or writes.

'I love your new jacket!' she said.
In your email you asked: 'Why don't you ever write to me?'

5.1B Reported speech

This is when we report something that has been said or written. If the report is after the time the thing was said or written, the verb form generally changes as follows:

	Direct speech	Reported speech
1	Present simple/continuous *She said, 'I'm meeting him on Friday.'*	Past simple/continuous *She **said she was meeting** him on Friday*
2	Past simple/continuous *'The class **finished** five minutes ago,' you said.*	Past perfect simple/continuous *You **said the class had finished** five minutes before.*
3	Present perfect simple/continuous *He told me, 'I've worked here for 20 years.'*	Past perfect simple/continuous *He **told me he had worked** there for 20 years.*
4	*will* *'I'**ll** tell him,' she said.*	*would* *She **said she would** tell him.*
5	*can* *My brother said, 'I **can** run a marathon.'*	*could* *My brother said he **could** run a marathon.*

1 Reported statements

Form

verb (+ *that*) + clause

We can use *say* and *tell* (and other verbs) to report statements. When we use *tell*, we use an object. When we use *say*, we don't use an object.

*You **said** (that) you were hungry.*
*He **told me** (that) he didn't love me.*
*They **said** (that) they would be late.*

2 Reported questions

Form

Wh- questions	
Direct speech	Reported speech
*'**What is Andrea doing**?'* she asked.	*She **asked** me **what Andrea was doing**.*
Question word + auxiliary verb + subject + verb	Question word + subject + verb

Yes/No questions	
Direct speech	Reported speech
*'**Do you like** coffee?' he asked.*	*He **asked** me **if/whether I liked** coffee.*
Auxiliary verb + subject + verb	*If* (or *whether*) + subject + verb

5.2 Phrasal verbs

- A phrasal verb is a verb together with one or more particles (e.g. *up, down, with,* etc.) that has a different meaning from the verb on its own.

  *He **gave up** playing football when he hurt his knee.*
  *I can't **put up with** the noise from next door any more.*

- There are four kinds of phrasal verbs that we use in different ways. Use information in dictionaries to help you tell which type a phrasal verb is.

1 Intransitive

- No object needed
- Shown in the dictionary as: [I]

> **break down** *phr v* [I] stop working (a car or machine)

*My car has **broken down** again!* ✓
~~My car has broken down it again!~~

2 Transitive and separable

- An object is necessary
- Shown in the dictionary as: [T]
- We can put the object between the main verb and the particle
- Shown in the dictionary as:
  e.g. *get **sth** across, put **sb** up*
  (sth = *something* / sb = *somebody*)

> **get sth across** *phr v* [T] to be able to make someone understand an idea or piece of information

*She **got** the message **across** quickly and clearly.* ✓
*She **got across** the message quickly and clearly.* ✓

3 Transitive and inseparable

- An object is necessary
- Shown in the dictionary as: [T]
- We can't put the object between the main verb and the particle
- Shown in the dictionary as:
  e.g. *look for **sth/sb***

> **look for** sth/sb *phr v* [T] try to find something or somebody using your eyes

*I've **looked for** my keys everywhere.* ✓
~~I've looked my keys for everywhere.~~

4 Transitive and inseparable with two particles

- An object is necessary
- Shown in the dictionary as: [T]
- We can't put the object between the main verb and the particles
- Shown in the dictionary as:
  e.g. *come down with **sth**, get on with **sb***

> **get on with** sb *phr v* [T] have a friendly relationship with somebody

*I **get on with** my brother.* ✓
~~I get my brother on with.~~

UNIT 6

6.1 The future

a) Forms
will + infinitive
going to + infinitive
present continuous
present simple

b) Use

1 We use *will* + infinitive for predicting something that we know or believe something about.

   *I think Brazil **will win** the next football World Cup.* (I know they are a very good team.)

2 We use *going to* + infinitive for predicting something that we can see, feel or hear some evidence about now.

   *I'm **going to be** sick.* (I feel awful now.)

Note: We can't use the present continuous in this case.

3 We use *will* + infinitive to talk about decisions made at the moment of speaking (sudden decisions).

Decision: help/ don't help?

I'll carry that for you.

PAST   NOW   FUTURE

Note: We can't use *going to* + infinitive in this case.

4   We use *going to* + infinitive to talk about decisions made before the moment of speaking (plans and intentions).

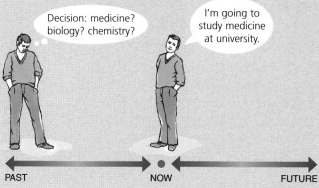

Note: We can't use *will* + infinitive in this case.

5   We use the present continuous to talk about plans and arrangements (things that have already been decided).

I'm meeting Jenny at 8 o'clock on Friday.

Note: We can't use *will* + infinitive in this case.

6   We use the present simple to talk about timetables and programmes.

His train leaves at 10.35.

UNIT 7

7.1 Requests (*can, could, would*)

a) We can make requests using *can, could* and *would*. *Could* and *would* are usually a little more polite than *can*.

1   *Can I/you* + infinitive without *to*
    ***Can I have** a cup of coffee, please?*

2   *Could I/you* + infinitive without *to*
    ***Could you say** that again, please?*

3   *Would you* + infinitive without *to*
    ***Would you lend** me your phone, please?*

b) We can make positive responses to requests using:
OK.   That's fine.
Yes, of course.   No problem.

c) When we make negative responses to requests we usually give a reason.
Sorry, I haven't finished reading it.
Sorry, someone's sitting there.

7.2 Obligation (*must/mustn't, have to/don't have to*)

We use *must, mustn't* and *have to* to express strong obligation and necessity.
We use *don't have to* to express lack of obligation.

1   *must*
    We use *must* to talk about present and future strong obligations and necessities that come from the speaker.
    *I **must go** to the dentist next week.*

2   *mustn't*
    We use *mustn't* to tell people **not** to do things.
    *You **mustn't tell** anyone.*

3   *have to*
    We use *have to* to talk about strong obligations that don't come from the speaker.
    *You **have to pay** to use Internet cafés.*

4   *don't have to*
    We use *don't have to* to talk about a lack of obligation in the present or future.
    *You **don't have to decide** now – tell me later.*

UNIT 8

8.1 Present perfect simple

a) Form
    have/has + past participle

b) Use

1   Indefinite past

We use the present perfect simple to talk about experience, that is things that have happened at some time in our lives. The time that the action happened is **indefinite** (unknown or unimportant).

*She's **met** him before.*
***Have you ever been** to Italy?*

Contrast:
Present perfect simple

*I've **seen** that film.*

With:
Past simple:

*I **saw** that film last Saturday.*

2 Unfinished past

We use the present perfect simple:

1 when we are describing situations that have continued from some time in the past until now.

   *My mother **has lived** in Athens for 30 years.*
   *I've **known** my best friend since I was fourteen.*
   *How long **have you had** your watch?*

   Contrast …

   *I've **lived** in Madrid for five years.* (present perfect simple)

   with …

   *I **live** in Madrid now.* (present simple)

2 when we are describing repeated actions that have continued from some time in the past until now.

   *I've **sent** fifteen emails this week.*
   *He's **phoned** his girlfriend every day for two months.*

3 when we are describing recent events.

   *I've **had** three cups of coffee so far today.*
   *He's **missed** his class six times this month.*

8.2 *Ever, never, already, yet, just*

We use *ever, never, already* and *yet* with the present perfect (not the past simple).

1 We use *ever* to talk about at *any* time in your life. It comes before the main verb (usually in questions).

   *Have you **ever** grown your own food?*

2 *Never* comes before the main verb.

   *I've **never** been on an aeroplane.*

3 *Already* means that something happened sooner than expected. It comes before the main verb.

   *We've **already** bought the tickets.*

4 *Yet* means *until now* and shows that the speaker expects something to happen. It comes at the end of the sentence (usually in questions and negative sentences).

   *We haven't thought about it **yet**.*
   *Have you thought about it **yet**?*

5 *Just* means that something happened a short time ago. It comes before the main verb.

   *I've **just** spoken to Amanda.*

UNIT 9

9.1 Relative pronouns and clauses

The most common relative pronouns are:

who: to refer to people
which: to refer to things
that: to refer to either people or things
whose: the possessive of *who* and *which*
when: used after nouns referring to time
where: used after nouns referring to place

1 Defining relative clauses

● We use defining relative clauses to define or identify a noun. They tell us exactly which person, thing, time or place we are talking about.
● No commas are used.
● Defining relative clauses are common in informal speech.
● We can use *that* to refer to things. *That* can also be used in informal speech to refer to people.
● We don't usually use *whom* in defining relative clauses.
   *Daniel is the man **who is wearing the hat**.*
   *That's the woman **whose bag was stolen**.*
   *What's the name of the place **where you went on holiday**?*
   *Here's the book **that you lent me**.*
   *This is the friend **that I told you about**.*

2 Non-defining relative clauses

● We use non-defining relative clauses to give extra information. They tell us more about a person, thing, time or place that is already identified.
● Commas are used before and after the relative clause.
● Non-defining relative clauses are generally more formal and more common in writing.
● We don't usually use *that* in non-defining relative clauses.
● We can use *whom* instead of *who* when we are referring to the object in non-defining relative clauses. *Whom* is more formal than *who*.
   *Rio de Janeiro, **where I lived for three years**, is a very beautiful city.*
   *On Friday, **when my exams are over**, I'm going to Jane's party.*
   *Elizabeth, **who is talking to your brother**, looks very upset.*
   *I went to that new restaurant, **which I really loved**.*
   *My teacher, **whom** I like very much, is leaving today.*

UNIT 10

10.1 Conditionals

1 Zero conditional

a) Form

If + present simple + present simple in the main clause

b) Use

To talk about what always happens.

*If you **eat** too much, you **get** fat.*
*If you **shout** at Charlie, he **starts** crying.*

2 First conditional

a) Form

If + present simple + *will* for future in the main clause

b) Use

To talk about what may possibly happen.

*If you **go** to the party, you**'ll see** Michael.*
*You**'ll be** tired tomorrow if you **don't go** to bed now.*

3 Second conditional

a) Form

If + past simple + *would, could*, etc. in the main clause

We can use *were* instead of *was* after *if*. In a formal style, *were* is more common than *was*.

b) Use

To talk about something:

1 which is unreal, untrue or imagined

   *If I **was** taller, I**'d be able** to reach that shelf.*
   *If I **were** taller, I**'d be able** to reach that shelf.*
   *If I **knew** her phone number, I**'d give** it to you.*

2 which will probably not happen in the future.

   *If I **lived** to be 100, I**'d have** a big party.*
   *What **would** you **do** if you **won** the lottery?*

4 Third conditional

a) Form

If + past perfect + *would have* + past participle in the main clause

b) Use

To talk about past situations that did not happen.

*If I**'d known** you were coming, I**'d have cooked** a proper meal.*
*If you **had been** kinder to her, she **wouldn't have left.***

UNIT 11

11.1 Making comparisons

There are three types of comparison. We can compare things:

a) to a higher degree (comparative form + *than*)

   *Maths is **more difficult than** biology.*

b) to the same degree (*as ... as*)

   *Chemistry is **as boring as** physics.*

c) to a lower degree (with *less* + *than*).

   *Geography is **less difficult than** algebra.*

11.1A Comparative and superlative forms of adjectives

1 One-syllable adjectives
   Add *-er* and *-est* to form the comparative and superlative of one-syllable adjectives.

   *My mum is **older than** my dad.*
   *My brother is **the tallest** person in my family.*

   With one-syllable adjectives:
   - that end in a vowel + a consonant, double the consonant, e.g. *fat, fatter, fattest; big, bigger, biggest*.
   - that end in *-e*, add *-r* and *-st*, e.g. *late, later, latest*.

2 Two-syllable adjectives
   Use *more* and *most* with two-syllable adjectives.

   *This book is **more boring than** that one.*
   *Jerry is **the most careful** driver I know.*

   With two-syllable adjectives ending in *-y*:
   replace the *-y* with *-i*, e.g. *easy, easier, easiest*.

3 Three-syllable adjectives
   Use *more* and *most* with three-syllable adjectives.

   *I think Paris is **more beautiful than** London.*
   *She's **the most important** person in the company.*

11.1B Irregular comparative and superlative adjectives

These are the most common irregular forms:
good, better, best
bad, worse, worst
far, further, furthest

*La Pizzeria is **better than** La Taverna, but La Trattoria is **the best**.*
*Peter's tennis is **worse than** Mark's, but mine is **the worst**.*
*Gina lives **further** from school **than** me, but Magda lives **the furthest** away.*

11.2 Advice (*should* and *ought to*)

- We use *should* and *Why don't you ...?* to give advice. We can also use *ought to*, but it is less common.

  *You look very tired. You **should** go to bed early tonight.*
  ***Why don't you** go to the doctor?*
  *You **ought to invite** Maria to the party.*

- We can use *should* in the negative.

  *You **shouldn't eat** so much – it's not good for you.*

- We don't usually use *ought to* in the negative. We can use it with *I don't think ...*

  ~~You oughtn't to spend so much money.~~
  *I **don't think** you **ought to spend** so much money.*

- We can also use *should* and *ought to* to talk about obligations and duties.

  *You **should** tell Dan if you know where his keys are.*
  *You **ought to** phone you mother more often.*

UNIT 12

12.1 Ability

a) Form

1. After *can* and *could* we use the infinitive (without *to*) of other verbs.

   *She can **sing** really well.*
   *I couldn't **reach** the shelf.*

2. With *can* and *could*, questions and negatives are made without *do/does*.

   ***Can you** swim?*
   *I couldn't **read** until I was seven.*

3. We use *be able to* in the past, the present and the future, by changing the verb *be*.

   Past: *He **was** able to finish the race.*
   Present: *She **is** able to read books in French.*
   Future: *I'**ll be** able to understand computers when I finish the course.*

b) Use

We use *can*, *could* and *be able to* to talk about ability. *Could* is not only used as the past of *can*. We also use *could* and *can* for requests (see Unit 7).

1. *can*
   We use *can* to talk about present and future ability.

   *She **can speak** four languages.*
   *I **can't finish** it before Friday.*

2. *could*
   We use *could* to talk about general past ability.

   *He **could ride** a bike when he was four.*
   ***Could you use** a computer when you were eight?*

3. *be able to*
   We use *am/are/is able to* to talk about present ability.

   *She **is able to remember** all her friends' phone numbers.*

   We use *will be able to* to talk about future ability.

   *I'**ll be able to buy** a new car when I get a pay rise.*

   We use *was/were able to* to say that somebody managed to do something on one occasion (usually something that was not easy).

   *He **was able to finish** the race in less than fifteen minutes.*

Note: We can't use *could* in this case.

12.2 *Used to* (past habits and states)

a) Form

Positive statements: *used to* + infinitive
Negative statements: *didn't use to* + infinitive
Questions: *Did you/she/they*, etc. + *use to* + infinitive

b) Use

We use *used to* to talk about past habits and states that don't occur now or no longer exist.

*I **used to play** the piano but now I don't.*
*He **didn't use to speak** Spanish but now he speaks it fluently.*
*They **used to live** near here but they've moved.*

UNIT 13

13.1 *Like* as a verb and as preposition

1. *like* as a verb
   a) *like* + *-ing* (= enjoy doing)
      *I **like going** to English classes because you can meet different people.*

   b) *would like* + (object) + infinitive with *to* is used as a polite way of saying *want*. It refers to the future.
      ***Would you like to go** out for lunch tomorrow?*
      *I'**d like you to see** my new flat soon.*

2 *like* as a preposition

When we use *like* as a preposition, it means *similar to* or *in the same way as*.

He really **looks like** his father.

Listen! It **sounds like** someone is calling for help.

13.2 Short answers

1 Agreeing

We use *so*, *neither* and *nor* when we want to agree with what someone says.

1 We use *so* with a positive auxiliary verb when both statements are positive.

I **like** chocolate. **So do I.**

Mariana **comes** to work by bus. **So does Julio.**

He **can play** tennis very well. **So can you.**

Ricky **will be** back at 6.30. **So will I.**

2 We use *neither* or *nor* with a positive auxiliary verb when both statements are negative.

I **don't like** chocolate. **Nor do I.**

I **haven't finished** my lunch. **Nor have I.**

She **can't speak** French. **Nor can I.**

I'm **not going** to the party. **Neither is Costas.**

Note: We can't use a negative auxiliary verb with *neither* or *nor*.

2 Disagreeing

When we disagree with what someone says, we can use short answers.

1 When the first statement is positive, the second statement is negative.

I **like** chocolate. **I don't.**

I'd **like to go** to the moon. **I wouldn't.**

They **are arriving** at 6 o'clock. **Jack isn't.**

2 When the first statement is negative, the second statement is positive.

I **don't like** chocolate. **I do.**

She **can't play** the guitar. **I can.**

Paulo **will be** late. **Anya won't.**

Note: We only use auxiliary verbs in the short answers. We can't use main verbs.

UNIT 14

14.1 Countable and uncountable nouns

1 Countable nouns can be used with:

- a singular or plural verb
  My **car is** in the garage.
  Three **people were standing** at the door.

- *a/an* for singular sentences
  She's got **a coat** and **an umbrella**.

- *some* for plural positive sentences
  I bought **some boots**.

- *any* for plural negative sentences and questions.
  I haven't got **any sandwiches** left.
  Are there **any books** on the table over there?

2 Uncountable nouns:

- always use a singular verb
  Accommodation is very expensive in London.

- never use *a/an*
  I want ~~an~~ information about flights.

- can use *some* for positive sentences
  I need **some advice** about how to change money.

- can use *any* for negative sentences and questions.
  There **isn't any bread** left.
  Have you got **any luggage**?

The following are common uncountable nouns:
accommodation, advice, bread, English (and all other languages), *fruit, furniture, information, luggage, rice* (and all other grains and cereals), *spaghetti* (and all other pasta), *traffic, travel*

Some nouns have both countable and uncountable uses:
paper / a paper (= a newspaper)
water / a water (= a glass of water)
coffee / a coffee (= a cup of coffee)
cake / a cake
chocolate / a chocolate

14.2 Articles

1 We use the indefinite article, *a/an* for:

- single countable nouns mentioned for the first time
  There's **a big tree** over there.
  Would you like **a sandwich**?
- Jobs.
  He's **an engineer**.
  I like being **a teacher**.

2 We use the definite article, *the*, for:

- previously mentioned nouns
  *There's a big tree over there. Let's sit under **the tree** to have our picnic.*
  *I made myself a sandwich and went to the fridge to get a drink. By the time I turned round **the sandwich** had gone.*

- when there's only one of something.
  *It's very cloudy tonight – I can't see **the moon**.*
  *When I was in Paris I went up **the Eiffel Tower**.*

3 We use no article for:

- most languages, names, streets, towns, cities, countries (except **the USA, the UK**)
  *She can speak **Spanish** and **Portuguese** fluently.*
  *This is **Tina**, my best friend.*
  *Let's go to **Oxford Street** this afternoon.*
  *He's just moved to **Manchester**.*
  *She's lived in **Australia** for ten years.*
  *I'm thinking of going to **the USA**.*

- uncountable nouns, plural nouns and abstract nouns
  *We need **bread**, **cheese** and **wine**.*
  ***Accommodation** in London is very expensive.*
  *I like **bananas** but I don't like **apples**.*
  *We've got **chickens** and **pigs** on our farm.*
  *He was up all night with **worry**.*
  *You need **patience** to be a teacher.*

UNIT 15

15.1 The passive (past and present)

a) Form

Appropriate tense of *be* + past participle

Present simple:
*English **is spoken** in many countries.*

Present continuous:
*My computer **is being repaired** at the moment.*

Past simple:
*That letter **was sent** by express post.*

Past continuous:
*The shop was closed because it **was being cleaned**.*

b) Use

The passive is used to talk about processes, actions and events:
a) when the process is more important than the person who did it (the agent),
b) when we don't know who did it.
  *Rare animals **are found** in this area.*
  *A lot of coffee **was exported** from Brazil last year.*
  *The exam results **were sent** yesterday.*

We can include the agent (who did it) in a passive sentence if it adds extra interesting information. We usually include it at the end of the sentence using *by*:

*My wedding dress was handmade **by my mother**.*
~~My wedding dress was handmade **by someone**.~~
*The thieves were arrested **by several policemen with guns**.*
~~The thieves were arrested **by a policeman**.~~

15.2 Causative *have* and *get*

a) Form

have + object + past participle
(this is the most common form)

get + object + past participle
(this form is also possible when people are speaking informally)

b) Use

We use *to have something done* to say that someone else did something for you. This is usually because you wanted them to and often means you paid for it, but it can sometimes be used when you didn't want them to do it.

*I **had my hair cut** yesterday.*
*She's **going to have her computer repaired** tomorrow.*
*Let's **get the car checked** before we go on holiday.*
*I **had my bag stolen** at the market yesterday.*

Writing reference

INDEX

SECTION A

1 What is a sentence?

1 All sentences must have SUBJECT + VERB (+ OBJECT) = SVO

Subject	Verb	Object
Simon	laughed.	
They	apologised.	
Claire	caught	the ball.
I	ate	an apple.

2 We can add adverbs, adjectives, etc. to the basic SVO sentence.

Examples:
- *She is very kind.*
- *Antonia is studying in her bedroom.*
- *At first, they were surprised.*
- *She put the book in her bag.*
- *For example, I go swimming every Saturday.*

3 You can link SVO sentences using conjunctions like *and, or, so, but*, etc. No comma is needed.

Examples:
- *They went shopping **and** they had a great time!*
- *We can stay here **or** we can go to my house.*
- *She wasn't very well **so** she went to bed.*
- *I like tea **but** I never drink coffee.*

4 You can also link SVO sentences using conjunctions like *because, although, after, when*, etc. The clause that begins with the conjunction can go first or second. Notice the punctuation.

Examples:
- ***Although** it was raining, she went jogging.*
- *She went jogging **although** it was raining.*
- ***After** they left, everyone had a good time.*
- *Everyone had a good time **after** they left.*

Note: We can't link SVO sentences with a comma. We must use a linking word.
- *~~I like listening to music, it's relaxing.~~*
- *I like listening to music. It's relaxing.*

or
- *I like listening to music **because** it's relaxing.*

Task

Six of the following are incorrect. Correct the mistakes.

1 Martin bought her a present. Although it wasn't her birthday.

2 I'll phone you when I arrive.

3 She's very lazy. Sleeps, watches television all day.

4 I think he's playing in the garden or he's watching TV.

5 After it rained the sun came out.

6 The hotel where we stayed was great. Because it was very comfortable.

7 I was very bored, I left.

8 I do lots of sport. Basketball, tennis and football last weekend.

2 Punctuation

1 Capital letters

We use capital letters:

a) at the beginning of a new sentence, e.g. *We went for a pizza first. Then we went back to Marta's house.*

b) for the names of particular things:
   people, e.g. *Richard*
   countries, e.g. *Spain*
   nationalities, e.g. *Greek*
   days and months, e.g. *Monday, October*
   places, e.g. *Oxford Street*
   titles, e.g. *The Times*

2 Full stops (.), question marks (?) and exclamation marks (!)

These are all used to end sentences. A new sentence that follows one of these has a capital letter.

Examples:
- *She bought a new computer yesterday.*
- *I can't believe you didn't tell me!*
- *Why were you so late? We waited for ages.*

3 Commas (,)

We use commas:

a) after introductory phrases or clauses, e.g.
   At first, I thought he was joking.
   If I had enough money, I'd buy a new CD player.
   Since he was always late for school, his father bought him an alarm clock.

b) around added information, e.g.
   That man, who looks like my father, is my teacher.
   I gave him a sandwich, which he ate at once.

c) to separate items in a list, e.g.
   She likes playing volleyball, football, tennis and table-tennis.

d) to divide groups of words in a sentence so the meaning is clear, e.g.
   She got up, had a shower, made breakfast and drove to work.

4 Apostrophes (')

We use apostrophes:

a) when certain words are contracted, e.g.
   I'll be late tonight. We've been invited to a party.

b) to show possession, e.g.
   This is John's room.

5 Commas and quotation marks ('...') in direct speech

a) A comma is usually used between a reporting expression and direct speech, e.g.
   After he finished eating, he asked, 'When are you leaving?'

b) If the reporting expression comes after the direct speech, we usually put a comma before the final quotation mark, e.g.
   'I think you're making a mistake,' said Sam.

c) We use quotation marks (or 'inverted commas') when we quote direct speech. Single quotation marks ('...') are more common in British English. Double quotation marks ("...") are more common in American English.

Task

Read this extract from a letter. Then write it again with appropriate punctuation.

the other thing that happened at the weekend was that I saw michelle do you remember her she was my best friend at primary school her family who lived in the same street as my family moved to Manchester when I was 12 and I havent seen them since as soon as she saw me she said wow christina youve grown up we couldnt stop laughing

3 Paragraphs

1 What is a paragraph?

A paragraph consists of a number of sentences based on one main topic. It usually starts with a topic sentence (highlighted in the example below) which tells you what the paragraph is about. All the other sentences are about that topic. Sentences in a paragraph should be linked with reference words and linkers. The first sentence of a new paragraph begins on a new line. There will often be a space between paragraphs.

Example:

Then on Sunday we went on a bus trip to Cambridge. We had a fantastic time! First of all, the weather was great (which makes a nice change) and so it was lovely just walking around all the old colleges. At lunchtime, we went and had sandwiches by the river and some of us even went 'punting' on boats along the river. At one point, I thought I was going to fall in but just saved myself! We were all sorry to come home.

Did I tell you about Paulo? He's in my class at school and he came to Cambridge too. He'd been before so he could tell me lots of things about it. He's really interesting. We're thinking about doing some more weekend trips to different places.

2 Linking sentences in a paragraph

Sentences in a paragraph should be connected by:

- reference words, e.g. *he, they, this, that*, etc.
  Example: *Tom was very angry.* **He** *refused to come out of his bedroom.*

- parallel expressions
  Example: *Her **teacher** said Julie's homework was the best in the class. She was surprised because she didn't think **Mr Alexander** liked her.*

- linking words and expressions, e.g. *then, however, in addition*
  Example: *We walked to the bus stop.* **Then** *we waited an hour for a bus to come.*

3 Linking paragraphs

In a letter, composition, article or other extended piece of writing, try to link paragraphs to show how your ideas are developing. You can do this by:

a) using a linking expression

Example:

Simon arrived on Friday night. I picked him up from the station. He was only here until Monday morning but we did lots of interesting things over the weekend.
First of all, we caught a train to Oxford and spent Saturday morning looking round the colleges

b) using a word (or words) from the last sentence of one paragraph in the first sentence of the next paragraph

Example:

The Lottery has become very important to lots of people. They dream of changing their lives. They don't realise how small the chances of winning are. That's why I never buy a ticket. However, if I did buy a ticket and I won a million pounds on the Lottery, I think I'd want to travel the world.
Travel is something I love but have never really had the chance to do seriously.

c) using a parallel expression

Example:

People are becoming more and more aware that we need to protect our environment. They notice the strange changes in the weather. They know that the destruction of the ozone layer is a problem that is not going to go away.
This issue must be looked into by all governments ...

Task

Begin this paragraph with an appropriate topic sentence. Then, complete spaces 2–4 with possible linking expressions.

(1) ....
First of all we visited the Eiffel Tower. (2) .... we went to the Louvre and saw the Mona Lisa. (3) .... we went shopping and bought lots of presents for the rest of the family!
(4) ....,
we had a fantastic meal in a restaurant on the Champs-Elysées before catching the train home.

---

4 Making your writing interesting

1 Introductions

In stories, a good introduction will set the scene, use interesting vocabulary and introduce the people in the story. Above all, it will make the reader want to continue reading.

Example:
Jessica and Sasha were sitting under a tree in the middle of some mountains. It was raining hard. They both knew they were completely lost but neither of them wanted to admit it.

2 Vocabulary

To keep the interest of your reader, it is important to use a good range of vocabulary. For example, don't always use words like *nice* and *good*. Think of more interesting adjectives and adverbs, e.g. *delicious, marvellously*, etc. that describe exactly what you mean.

> **Task**
>
> Rewrite the paragraph below replacing the underlined words with more interesting and precise vocabulary. (You may wish to use some of the following words: *delicious, fantastic, wonderful, lovely, marvellous, great*.)
>
> We arrived at the hotel yesterday and it's really <u>nice</u>. We have a <u>nice</u> room with a <u>good</u> view of the sea. This morning we had a <u>nice</u> breakfast and then went to the beach. There is a <u>good</u> programme of social activities and tomorrow we are going to visit some nearby ruins.

3 Varied sentences

Try to write longer sentences. Join the parts of the sentence with linking expressions, e.g. *because, so, although*, etc.

Example: *I went to the library because I needed some books for an essay.*

> **Task**
>
> Make one sentence from the pairs of sentences below using the word in brackets.
>
> 1 The film had my favourite actor in it. I didn't enjoy it. (*but*)
>
> 2 I took my umbrella. It was raining. (*because*)
>
> 3 She didn't answer all the questions. She passed the exam. (*although*)
>
> 4 I waited for a long time for the bus. I was late for school. (*so*)
>
> 5 Tom met his friend Steve. They decided to go bowling. (*and*)

4 Reported speech

You can include the words of other people in your writing. This adds interest and variety. When you do this, you are using **reported speech**, e.g. *The policeman said that they needed to get the man to hospital.*

(**Note:** In indirect speech there are various changes of verb forms, pronouns, etc.)

> **Task**
>
> Read the paragraph below and match the reported speech (1–3) to the spaces (a–c).
>
> 1 I told him we had to have it in the hotel where they got married.
>
> 2 he asked me what I thought
>
> 3 my dad told me that he wanted to arrange a surprise party for my mum.
>
> When I got home (a) .... He said he was going to invite all her friends. He wasn't sure where we should have the party and (b) .... I knew immediately. (c) .... He thought it was a brilliant idea. I can't wait for it to happen now!

5 Formal and informal language

The style of your writing depends on:

1 **who** you are writing to

2 **why** you are writing.

You will, for example, use an **informal** style to write to good friends but a **formal** style to write a job application letter.

Here are some examples of formal and informal language.

Formal language

Examples	Comments
I would be very grateful if you could send me information regarding your summer courses.	Long sentences. Full forms of verbs, e.g. *I would*
We would appreciate a reply as soon as possible.	Formal vocabulary, e.g. *appreciate* rather than *like*

Informal language

Examples	Comments
I think she's making a big mistake, don't you?	Contractions, e.g. *she's* Question tags, e.g. *don't you?*
I hope you're OK.	Sounds like spoken language. Everyday vocabulary, e.g. *OK*

Task

Read the formal letter below. The writer is asking for information. Decide which of the alternatives are most appropriate.

Dear *John,/Sir or Madam,*

I thought I'd drop you a line about/I am writing in response to your advertisement in Tuesday's 'Guardian' newspaper. *I would be very grateful/It would be great* if you could send me more information about your summer language school.

Can't wait to hear from you!/I look forward to hearing from you.

Yours faithfully,/Love,

Stuart Henderson

6 Spelling

1 Adding syllables

a) doubling the final consonant
   We often double the final consonant in one-syllable words if they end in a vowel followed by a consonant, e.g. *big – bigger, stop – stopping, plan – planned*.

b) words ending in *-e, -ee* and *-ie*
   We usually drop the final *-e* in words when an ending with a vowel (e.g. *-ing, -ous*, etc.) is added, e.g. *make – making, love – loving*.
   The final *-e* is not dropped from words ending in *-ee*, e.g. *see – seeing, agree – agreement*.
   We change *-ie* to *-y* before *-ing*, e.g. *lie – lying*.

c) Words ending in *-y*
   When adding an ending, we usually change *-y* to *-i*, e.g. *happy – happiness, easy – easier*.
   We do not change *-y* to *-i* before *i*, e.g. *try – trying*.

2 Plurals

We often make the plural of nouns by adding *-s*, e.g. *cat – cats*.
However, we add *-es* after words which end in *-s, -ss, -sh, -ch* and *-x*, e.g. *bus – buses; match – matches*.

Here are some irregular plurals: *a child – children; a knife – knives; a tooth – teeth; a mouse – mice; a woman – women; a baby – babies; a person – people; a sheep – sheep*.

3 Spelling and pronunciation

a) homophones
   These are words which are pronounced the same but spelled differently:
   mail – male; break – brake; pour – poor; cereal – serial; heel – heal; peace – piece; stationary – stationery; toe – tow; minor – miner

Task

Find the different meanings of the words in the pairs above. Check in a dictionary.

b) silent letters

Here are some common words where the letters in brackets are not pronounced:

choc(o)late, bus(i)ness, diff(e)rent, rest(au)rant, ev(e)ning, comf(or)table, int(e)resting, veg(e)table, secret(a)ry, temp(e)rature, cu(p)board, i(s)land, (p)sychology, We(d)nesday, (k)nife, forei(g)n, san(d)wich

4 Improving your spelling

a) Use a dictionary.

A good dictionary will give you a lot of information about new words, including: the correct spelling, the meaning, the pronunciation, examples in context, grammatical information, other forms of the word.

> **dic•tion•a•ry** /ˈdɪkʃənəri $ ˈdɪkʃəˌneri/ *noun, plural* **dictionaries** a book that gives a list of words in alphabetical order, with their meanings in the same or another language: *If you don't understand a word, look it up in a dictionary.*

b) Keep a personal spelling list of words you find difficult. Add to it each time you meet a new word which is difficult to spell. Revise your list regularly. Get someone else to test you on the correct spelling of the words.

c) Learn key words related to a topic.

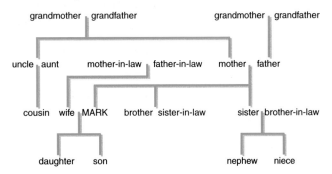

d) Keep a vocabulary notebook.

For an example, see Unit 2, Vocabulary 2 page 17.

7 Planning your writing

Follow these stages before you write.

1 Brainstorm

One of the biggest problems when writing is having enough ideas. *Brainstorming* means writing down as many ideas, words or phrases connected with a task or topic as you can think of. (You don't have to write complete sentences when you do this.)

2 Select and prioritise

Choose the best ideas and tick them. Remember that in an exam you will only be able to write a certain number of words.

3 Write a plan

Plan how many paragraphs you will have and the main subject of each of your paragraphs. Organise your ideas into separate paragraphs. This will help you to write a good letter, story, etc. and avoid having to make lots of changes.

Task

- Your English teacher has asked you to write a story.
- Your story must begin with this sentence: *Jo woke up feeling a little bit anxious.*
- Write your story in about 100 words.

Key questions	Ideas
Background: Who are the main characters? What are they like?	Jo – 16-year-old girl. Wants to be an actor.
Events: Where and when did the story take place? What happened? Why? How?	At home, then school. Big performance of a a play. Jo = main actor. Great success.
Ending: How did the story finish? How did everyone feel?	Jo's picture in local newspaper. Everyone excited and happy.

Task

- This is part of a letter you receive from an English penfriend.

> In your next letter, please tell me all about your favourite free-time activity. Why do you like doing it?

- Now you are writing a letter to this penfriend.
- Write your letter in about 100 words.

Dear (first name) *Mica,*

(Refer to their last letter or say sorry for not writing.) *Thanks for your last letter. It was great to hear all your news! I'm glad you had a good holiday.*

(Respond to any questions in their letter.) *You asked about my favourite free-time activity. In fact, at the moment, I'm spending a lot of time playing tennis. There are some tennis courts near my house and I'm having lessons from a tennis coach. I'm really enjoying it and usually play three or four times a week. It's great when it's nice weather but not so nice when it rains!*

(Finish your letter by asking a question, requesting news, etc.) *I hope you are well. Write soon and tell me what's happening!*

(Closing expression) *Best wishes,*

(Signature) *Claire*

8 Editing your writing

When writing any kind of text (letter, story, article, etc.), you must check that you have thought about these points:

Paragraphing
- Have you written 2–4 paragraphs?
- Does each paragraph have a topic sentence?
- Are the sentences in each paragraph on the subject of the topic sentence?
- Are some of the sentences linked with linking expressions?
- Are the paragraphs linked with parallel expressions, etc.?

Interest
- In your story is there an interesting introduction which sets the scene and makes the reader want to continue reading?
- Is there a good range of vocabulary?
- Are the sentences varied with good use of linking expressions?

Style
- Have you thought about who you are writing for?
- Is your writing appropriately formal or informal?

Accuracy
- Have you written complete sentences?
- Is your spelling and punctuation correct?
- Have you made any basic grammar mistakes?

Answering the question
- Have you done everything the task asked you to do?
- Have you written the correct number of words?

Task

Look at the task and letter below. There are some mistakes in the letter. The teacher has indicated the mistakes and where they are. Decide what the teacher's notes mean. Then correct the mistakes.

- At the weekend you went to a concert with some friends.
- Now you are writing to tell an English-speaking friend about the day.
- Tell him/her why you enjoyed the concert and what you did afterwards.
- Write about 100 words.

Dear Emily,

I must tell you ∧ the concert I go to last week. It was wonderful. Travis was performing. I really like this group and some freinds bought me tickets for my birthday. I was too happy. We were standing right at the front of the stage. At the end of ∧ concert we got some Autographs from the band! Afterwards we went to a great pizza restaurant. We had a wonderful time and after the pizza they brought us a huge chocalate birthday cake and sang 'Happy Birthday'!

Can't wait to hearing all your news.

Yours faithfully,

Suzanne

SECTION B

◼ 1 Informal letters

(For work on informal letters see pages 19, 27, 63 and 96.)

Task

Next month you are going to have birthday party. Now you are writing to invite an English-speaking friend to come to the party. Tell him/her:

- when it will be
- what will happen
- about any travel arrangements
- you are looking forward to seeing him/her.

Write your letter in about 100 words.

> Start your first paragraph under the end of the opening line or under the beginning of the opening line.

> Do invent a name. Don't write *Dear Friend*.

> Do divide your letter into separate paragraphs.

> Do finish with an appropriate informal expression.

> Do use informal language.

Dear David,

    I'm just writing to let you know that I'm having a party on Saturday 24th March to celebrate my 16th birthday. It will be at my parents' house from about 8 p.m. and there'll be food and music.

    I'm not sure how you'll get here but if you come by train or bus, we can pick you up from the station. Just let us know what time you will arrive!

    I really hope you can come. It will be great to see you and hear all your news. I want to hear about your holiday in America!

Love,
Elena

Useful language

Opening

- *Dear X, Sorry not to have written sooner but ...*
- *Dear Y, Thanks for your letter. It was great to get all your news.*

Reasons for writing

- *I'm just writing to tell you ...*
- *I thought I'd write and let you know that ...*

Development

- *As well as that, I also ...*
- *Another thing is that ...*

Closing

- *Do write back soon and let me know all your news. Love, ...*
- *Looking forward to seeing you on the 17th. Best wishes, ...*

2 Stories

(For work on short stories see pages 11, 37, 41 and 105.)

Task

- You have decided to enter a competition in your school magazine.
- You have to write a short story starting with the sentence: *It all happened last summer.*
- Write your story in about 100 words.

> Do use different past tenses correctly.

It all happened last summer. I was having a holiday in the USA with a friend and we had decided to go white water rafting.

There were eight of us in a boat with a guide. He was very friendly and helpful. He told us where to sit and what to do. Then we started moving slowly down the river.

A short time later it was not so relaxing. The river was moving fast and suddenly a lot of water came into the boat. I slipped and fell over the side. I soon came to the surface but it was a bit of a shock!

> Do use interesting vocabulary like *white water rafting*. Don't write about a topic if you don't know specific words like *boat*, *guide*, etc.

> Do use phrases to show when things happened in your story, e.g. *then*, *suddenly*, *soon*, etc.

> Do have an interesting ending to your story.

Useful language

- **We had** arrive**d** at the hotel the previous night.
- **I was ly**ing on the beach, reading my book **when** it started to rain.
- **At first**, no one moved.
- **Then**, we went to look for Katie.
- **Suddenly**, a cat ran out into the road.
- **A little later**, I heard someone shouting.
- **Eventually**, the police arrived.

3 Compositions

(For work on compositions see page 77.)

Task

- You have been doing a class project on communication. Your teacher has asked you to write a composition giving your opinion on the following statement:

  It is a good thing for young people to have mobile phones.

- Write your composition in about 100 words.

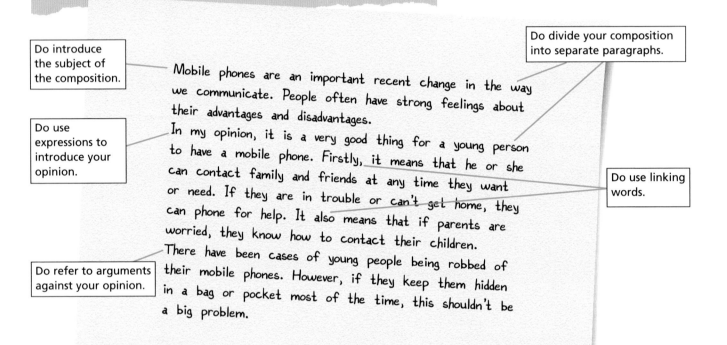

Do introduce the subject of the composition.

Do use expressions to introduce your opinion.

Do refer to arguments against your opinion.

Do divide your composition into separate paragraphs.

Do use linking words.

Mobile phones are an important recent change in the way we communicate. People often have strong feelings about their advantages and disadvantages.

In my opinion, it is a very good thing for a young person to have a mobile phone. Firstly, it means that he or she can contact family and friends at any time they want or need. If they are in trouble or can't get home, they can phone for help. It also means that if parents are worried, they know how to contact their children.

There have been cases of young people being robbed of their mobile phones. However, if they keep them hidden in a bag or pocket most of the time, this shouldn't be a big problem.

Useful language

Giving opinions

- **I think** that all children should learn two foreign languages at school.
- **In my opinion**, everyone should have a mobile phone.
- **As far as I'm concerned**, smoking in all public places should be banned.
- **From my point of view**, people should take more care of the environment.

Linking expressions of addition

- **I also** think that going to university should be free.
- **As well as that**, the government should reduce the cost of public transport.
- **In addition**, we are going to keep the school swimming pool open during the summer holidays.

Linking expressions of contrast

- Everyone agrees that we should eat more fruit and vegetables **but** it isn't always easy.
- Children want their parents to be interested in what they are doing. **However**, they also need freedom to make their own decisions.
- **Although** films can be very enjoyable, books are better at stimulating the imagination.

4 Reports

(For work on reports see pages 88 and 133.)

Task

As part of a class project, your teacher has asked you to write a report about how television in your country could be improved. Write your report in about 100 words.

Do use headings.

Do use formal language.

Do state facts. Don't give personal opinions until the conclusion.

Introduction

The aim of this report is to discuss briefly the good and bad points of television in my country.

Present situation

Television has two purposes in society, entertainment and education. Television in my country at present has a good variety of sports programmes, soaps, cartoons and films. However, in comparison with some other countries there are few good educational programmes especially for teenagers and children.

Conclusion and recommendations

Television plays a major part in the development of young people. Consequently, it is important that there are good educational programmes as well as entertainment. I believe there should be a better balance of the two.

Useful language

Introduction

- *The aim of this report is to ...*
- *This report is intended to ...*

Linking expressions of consequence

- **Therefore**, *the school should buy more computers for students to use.*
- *There are few leisure facilities for young people* **so** *they spend a lot of time watching TV.*
- **Consequently**, *fewer and fewer people travel by bus.*

Recommendations

- *It is important that ...*
- *I believe we should ...*
- *I recommend that we ...*

5 Articles

(For work on articles see page 116.)

Task

- You have just seen the following advertisement:

> **Young People Today** magazine is looking for articles in answer to the question 'What makes a good friend?' We will publish some of the best articles next month.

- Write your article in about 100 words.

Do think of an interesting title.

Do use informal language.

Do try to 'talk' to your readers.

Do express your opinion.

A Friend For Life

We all have friends but obviously not all friends are the same! So, what makes a 'good friend?'

Let's start with an example. I got to know my best friend, Veronica, in primary school. We've both had some hard times since then. Last year I split up with my boyfriend and was very unhappy. A lot of my friends thought I was quite difficult and stopped calling me. Veronica didn't. She was always ready to talk when I needed to.

Many 'friends' come and go. Often they are there when everything is going OK but when life gets difficult they disappear. As far as I'm concerned a really good friend is someone who is always there for you.

Useful language

Talking to the reader

- *Do you have friends who have let you down?*
- *So, what would you do for your best friend?*

Informal language

- *Good friends always keep in touch.*
- *If there's a problem, talk it over.*

Communication activities

Unit 13, Vocabulary 1 Exercise 4 (p.110)

Unit 10, Vocabulary 2 Exercise 1 (p.86)

1

Well, me and my friend, Caroline, were on holiday in Australia. It was really hot and we'd been lying on this beautiful sandy beach for ages ... *well*, *anyway*, *then* we decided to go for a swim. *So*, we're walking into the water ... there are lots of other people around. *Then*, *just as* the water's about up to the top of my legs, I hear this screaming: 'Shark! Shark!' *Well*, I can tell you, everyone just started screaming and running for the beach! *Honestly*, I've never been so frightened in all my life. *In the end*, it turns out it was just a kid playing a joke ... *can you believe it*?

2

Have I told you about our cat, Twix? She's really funny. Just yesterday, I was sitting doing my homework in my dad's study with the door open ... *you know*, it goes out into the garden and the pond. *Anyway* ... Twix was out in the garden and was sitting on the edge of the pond. *Well*, you know there are fish in the pond ... *well*, so does Twix, and she loves to watch them. *So*, there she is, sitting, looking to see where the fish are. *Suddenly*, there's this great 'splosh' and this ball of wet fur flies past me and back into the house. She'd got just a bit too interested in the fish and fallen right in the pond. *Really*, *you know*, I just couldn't stop laughing!

3

OK well, I've got an even better horror story for you. *You see*, I was camping for the weekend with some friends. I'd woken up quite early and, *you know*, I was half asleep. *Anyway*, I was just about to put on my shoes before going off for a shower when I saw – in my shoe – the most enormous spider you have ever seen. It was huge and furry – I nearly fainted. I was in a complete panic. Just thinking about what would have happened if I hadn't been paying attention, it's too ... brrgghghh!

4

It was some time last year I think. I was going for a walk with my dad. We'd cut across some fields and got a bit lost. ... *Anyway*, *suddenly*, there in this field, we found ourselves staring into the eyes of this very very big, black bull. I'd never been quite so close to one before. I could feel myself go white with fear. I was paralysed. I couldn't move a muscle. *Eventually*, the bull seemed to lose interest and wandered off. *You cannot believe* how relieved we were!

Unit 12, Listening Exercise 2 (p.102)

Speaker 1: Hmmmm, that's a hard one but I actually have really strong memories of us all packing our suitcases, choosing what we could and couldn't take with us, filling up our old car and then driving off on a hot August day. Hours later, hot and tired, we'd arrive at this little place that we went to every year. We'd be greeted by Mrs Jenkins who ran it ... and then go up to our rooms. Straightaway, I used to unpack my case, put on my swimming costume and run down to the beach. The water used to be freezing but I didn't care. I loved it!

Unit 11, Speaking Exercise 3 (p.96)

How to survive a poisonous snake attack

1 Wash the bite with soap and water as soon as you can.

2 Keep the bitten area still and lower than the heart. This will slow the movement of poison.

3 Immediately wrap a bandage tightly two to four inches above the bite to help slow the poison.

4 Do **not** try to suck out the poison. It might enter your bloodstream.

How to survive an earthquake

1 If you are indoors, stay there. Get under a desk or table, or move into a doorway.

2 If you are outside, get into the open. Move away from buildings or anything else that might fall.

3 After the earthquake stops, check for injuries and apply the necessary first aid or look for help.

4 Put out any fires in your home or neighbourhood. Do not use matches – there may be gas leaks.

How to treat frostbite

1 Remove wet clothing and dress the area with warm, dry clothing.

2 Immerse frozen areas (generally fingertips, toes, nose, ears and cheeks) in warm water (100–105°F). If warm water is not available, wrap gently in warm blankets. (Avoid direct heat such as electric fires.)

3 Do not rub frostbitten skin.

4 Get medical treatment as soon as possible.

Unit 13, Vocabulary 1 Exercise 4 (p.110)

Unit 10, Speaking Exercise 4 (p.85)

1

Karen	So, what are we going to do tonight?
Andrew	Why don't we go to the Rainforest Café, you know, in the centre of town. It's supposed to feel like you really are in the rainforest with tropical birds, huge fishtanks, waterfalls ...
Tania	Oh no, I've just eaten ... not a café.
Simon	I'm not hungry either.
Andrew	Well, what about a film? How about the new Matt Damon then?
Karen	Yes, that's a good idea. I agree. Tania and Simon aren't hungry so let's go and see a film.

2

Tom	So, what are we going to do tonight?
Rob	Well, we could go round to Sarah's ...
Paula	All I know is that I'm hungry!
Kate	Me too!
Rob	And me!
Paula	So why don't we go for pizza?
Tom	I think you're right. We're all hungry so going for pizza is the best idea!